THE
MANAGER'S
DILEMMA

HOW TO EMPOWER YOUR
TEAM'S PROBLEM-SOLVING

IRIAL O'FARRELL

First published in the USA by
Evolution Consulting, 2021
Dublin, Ireland

ISBN: 978-1-8380731-4-5 (Paperback)

Printed in the USA by Kindle Direct Publishing, Seattle, Washington, USA

Cover by 100Covers
Interior Design by FormattedBooks.com

OTHER BOOKS BY THIS AUTHOR

Values—Not Just for the Office Wall Plaque:
How Personal and Company Values Intersect

The Performance Development Series:
SMART Objective Setting for Managers: A Roadmap

DEDICATION

To my big sisters, Lorraine, Dilis and Rowena, for
shaping me in so many different ways.

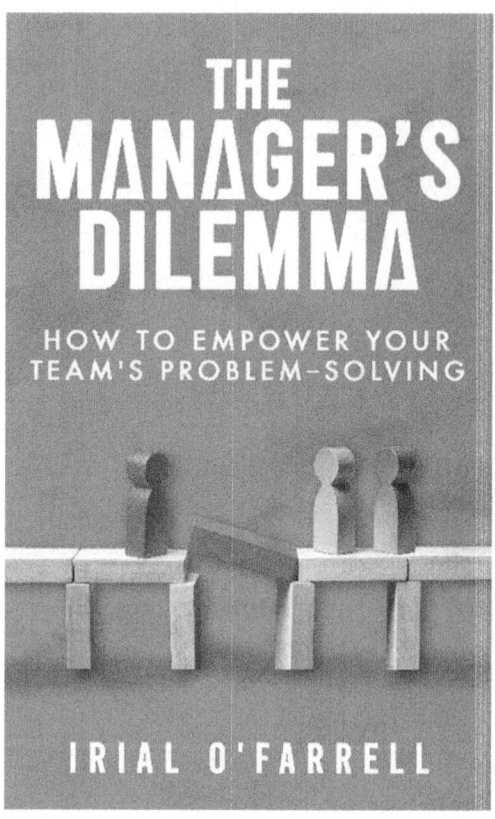

YOUR FREE GIFT

To make this book practical and relevant to your own situation, as you work through the chapters you'll be invited to consider how the ideas relate to your team. You might find it useful to have templates that you can save or print off and use, and keep all your answers in one place. To this end, I've included free gifts for your use.

Go to https://bit.ly/DilemmaFreeGifts to choose your free gift:

Manager's Problem-Solving Mindset Worksheet
Prompts-for-You Worksheet

CONTENTS

INTRODUCTION

While managing a Learning & Development (L&D) function in the financial funds industry, an incident occurred that took me by surprise. I was sitting at my desk when the L&D assistant manager came over to me to ask what she should do about some issue that needed to be resolved. Nearly twenty years later, I still remember pushing my chair back from the desk and swivelling it around to look up at her properly. All that was going through my head was, *Surely she knows the answer to that!* For someone who can talk the hind legs off a donkey, for once, words failed me. "Why?" you might wonder.

As we'll see in Chapter One, many managers wouldn't think twice about this question, even if they *did* think the person should know the answer. It definitely wouldn't make them pause for thought. Here's why I was so surprised—I knew, without a shadow of a doubt, that she knew the answer. What I couldn't understand was why she was asking me. Once recovered, I gave her the answer and off she went. However, the incident lodged in my mind.

I'm a great believer in reflection. Upon delivering a workshop or conducting a coaching session, specific conversations pique my interest and they tend to linger with me until I can fully make sense of them. This incident definitely caught my attention and I spent quite a bit of time figuring out what could possibly have prompted her to ask that question. It wasn't because she didn't know the answer, since I was convinced that she did know the answer. What could it possibly be? A conundrum indeed.

You'll be delighted to hear that my reflections did throw up some ideas and prompted a new approach to be used the next time the situation arose. Thankfully, the next time it happened, I actually managed to remember to apply the new approach. Within a couple of months, the approach had worked and the situation never arose again.

Job done, I didn't think too much about it until years later. I was mentoring a group of senior leaders. I can't remember the specific story that prompted my action but, as I listened, I realised that what they were describing was very similar to my experience. I thought I'd take a punt and throw my theory onto the table. I was curious to see if it would resonate with them or if it was just a blip in my own experience.

As I described my theory, I was getting a lot of nodding heads and comments such as, "Yes, that makes perfect sense", "Of course!" and, "Oh, I do that too!" type comments. Maybe there was something in this, after all! Over the next several years, I shared my theory with hundreds of managers. What became clear was that it really, really resonated with them.

From having worked with, and talked to, numerous managers, a definite trend was emerging. The majority of them were struggling with team members constantly interrupting them to ask a question or look for an answer. While the managers sensed that, *really*, these issues should have been resolved by the team members themselves, they didn't know how to break the dynamic. In the absence of an alternative, they found themselves sorting out the issues instead. As a result, the managers were getting overwhelmed as work, their own and their teams', piled up.

The managers knew they didn't like the dynamic but didn't know how to change it. The inevitable discussions that arose from sharing the theory led me to believe that hundreds of thousands of other managers must also grapple with this dynamic, which has prompted writing the book.

At this point, you're probably wondering *what* exactly my theory is. More importantly, how can the theory be applied to break the dynamic? You'll be delighted to read, dear readers, that this is the basis of this book and all will be revealed in good time. However, before we dive into the main body of the book, a few questions need to be answered.

WHO IS THIS BOOK'S IDEAL AUDIENCE?

This book is written for any manager that constantly has team members bringing issues, problems, or decisions to be made to them, which the manager thinks those individuals should be able to resolve for themselves. It's for managers suffering from "over-escalation", if you will. It is relevant for managers at all levels and for both operational and project-type work. So, if you run an operations team, a project team, or you have several levels of management reporting into you, you will benefit from applying the book's insights.

Some issues or problems require cross-functional discussion and decisions. Participants should attend such meetings with the requisite research completed and some ideas as to how to resolve them. This type of situation is beyond the scope of this book. However, if someone attends such a meeting and consistently tends to be a good problem-identifier (i.e. excels at pointing out the issues) rather than a good problem-solver (i.e. isn't contributing ideas to understanding the issues and finding suitable solutions), then their manager could take them aside and, using the content of this book, help them to develop their problem-solving skills to effectively contribute to such meetings.

IS THIS ONLY FOR TRADITIONAL TEAMS?

The book is written for managers of teams, whether that is a manager within a business-as-usual function or a project manager. By definition, agile and self-directed teams operate without a manager or team lead. As such, this book isn't specifically geared towards those types of teams.

Also, by definition, an agile or self-directed team is made up of team members who are competent in their areas of expertise. This implies that there are several behavioural competencies, core to the team's success, that all team members need to exhibit competence in. The ability to problem-solve is one of them. If a team member is struggling with their problem-solving, this book could be used within the team. It could be introduced in a book-club type format, i.e. everyone reads the book, in advance, and discusses its central ideas. The team could then collectively agree how they might approach preparing for and resolving issues and problems that fall within the team's remit.

WHAT IS MEANT BY PROBLEM-SOLVING?

This might seem like an odd point to include, but some people get quite agitated about the use of the word "problem". They perceive it to have negative connotations or interpret it as being "big problems" when really their team members only bring up minor issues.

Use of the word "problem-solving" in the book refers to any issue or problem that is delaying action being taken within the team and needs to be resolved. It might be quite a minor point or issue but, since there is uncertainty, somebody needs to make a call or provide direction.

From the manager's perspective, that "somebody" should really be someone within the team, but, instead, the issue is regularly escalated up to the manager, for them to make the call.

The words "problem" and "issue" will be used interchangeably.

DO I NEED TO HAVE READ *SMART OBJECTIVE SETTING FOR MANAGERS* BEFORE I READ THIS BOOK?

The short answer to this question is "No, you don't". The longer answer to this question is "You don't have to, but you would benefit immensely if you had read it."

While Chapter Four gives a quick overview of the SMART framework, the main purpose of this book is to explore the manager's dilemma and its impact on the team's performance. Then the book explores how to break the habit and develop individual team members to empower their problem-solving, thereby freeing up the manager. The overview chapter will cover out key points, to ensure readers who haven't read the SMART Objective Setting book can follow the approach I recommend for setting objectives.

However, if you are a people-manager, with responsibility for developing your team and their performance, you would benefit enormously from reading *SMART Objective Setting for Managers* to increase understanding of:

- the catch with SMART
- assumptions we carry into our conversations when agreeing objectives
- different types of objectives, including a detailed understanding of what a behavioural objective is and
- how to frame a behavioural-objective conversation

CAN THIS APPROACH ONLY BE USED DURING OBJECTIVE SETTING?

This is the second book in the Performance Development series. In terms of the Performance Management and Development Cycle, the book's content naturally sits in the behavioural developmental space, i.e. developing how individuals approach doing their work. In this case, specifically how to develop their problem-solving skills. During this book, we will use the SMART framework as a tool to tease out a specific individual's starting point and to put shape on a plan as to how we might approach developing their problem-solving skills.

In this case, the SMART framework is being used as a management preparation tool, to guide the manager. You, as the manager, will then have a choice as to how to implement the new approach. If you're heading into objective-setting season, it might make sense to introduce the new approach as a formal objective, tailored for each team member.

If you're reading this book and thinking, *I can't wait that long. I need to break this cycle now!* that's okay too. The same preparation still needs to be completed so that you are clear where the starting point is for coaching each team member. However, introducing the approach will be more informal, guided by the preparation done in the background.

In summary, this approach can be introduced at any time of the year. If it coincides with the objective-setting process, it is very easy to formally incorporate it into an individual objective. If it doesn't, the required developmental coaching can be provided on a more informal basis. Regardless of when it is introduced, analysis of each individual team member's starting point and preparation of their developmental coaching needs can be done. We are going to use the SMART framework to guide that preparation. With practice, you will be able to pinpoint exactly what an individual's issue is likely to be and which point to start coaching them from. In time, this will lessen the need to formally use SMART.

In addition, consideration needs to be given to how to communicate the changes in expectations. Chapter Thirteen will walk you through the various points to consider when introducing the new approach.

WILL THIS BOOK COVER OUT DIAGNOSTIC, PROBLEM-SOLVING, OR DECISION-MAKING TOOLS OR TECHNIQUES?

There are many books that deal with the processes, tools and techniques of problem-diagnosis, problem-solving and decision-making. This isn't one of those books. Managers typically tend to be very good at problem-solving and have learnt the typical tools and techniques used within their industry. However, when a person is naturally good at something, such as problem-solving, it can be difficult to recognise that not everyone finds it quite so easy. A team member may need direction, need to have their confidence built up or need help structuring their thinking.

For a manager, the process of recognising and diagnosing these individual needs is quite different to just sorting out the technical issue at hand. However, if the manager just continually sorts out the issues, the individual team members don't develop and are disempowered from taking ownership. This book is written specifically to help managers recognise the dynamics of problem-solving within their team and to help them to actively alter those dynamics.

By investing the time and effort into developing each team member's ability and confidence in resolving many of their own issues, the manager builds up and empowers their team. The reward is a high-performing team and a manager freed up to take on alternative opportunities within the company. Indeed, they may even informally become a self-directed team.

This book doesn't prescribe any specific diagnosis, problem-solving or decision-making tools and techniques. So, if your company uses Lean or 6Sigma tools or techniques, feel free to continue to use them. If you have a decision-making matrix, I can assure you, you'll still be using it by the end of this book. Whatever processes, tools and techniques you use to problem-solve, this book is based on the idea that you, as a manager, know how to solve problems within your industry.

Nor will this book differentiate between the two broad approaches to problem-solving, namely first principles vs. practical application. Again, it is assumed that whichever approach is most prevalent in your country, company, and team will automatically be enshrined into the approach you, as the manager, take with your team. For example, many Anglo-Saxon-based education systems, such as the USA, UK and Ireland, approach problem-solving from a practical-application perspective, i.e. what needs to get done to sort this out? On the other hand, many European-based education systems, such as France and Germany, tend to take the first-principles approach, i.e. what is it that we are seeking to achieve with this?

Rather, what this book *does* focus on is building the manager's knowledge and skills to recognise and diagnose each individual's developmental starting point and how to introduce the new approach.

WILL THIS BOOK COVER OUT THE MANAGER'S MINDSET ON PROBLEM-SOLVING?

Now we're talking. If you read *SMART Objective Setting for Managers*, you'll most likely remember that there was an entire chapter on the manager's "performance management" mindset. So, you won't be surprised to learn that we will be spending some time on the manager's mindset in this book too. This time, we'll focus on the manager's mindset in relation to problem-solving.

We will explore how the manager's mindset can contribute to the dynamic that is distracting them from focusing on their own work. We will consider how this mindset actually causes the manager to become part of the bottleneck. We will also discover what might be causing that mindset and explore some ways to shift it, so that the manager, and the team, gets different outcomes. In case you were wondering, getting the benefits of this book will require a bit of effort, but the rewards will be well worth the effort for all involved.

CAPTURING YOUR CURRENT "MANAGER'S MINDSET" WHEN RESPONDING TO ISSUES

In preparation for exploring this topic, I invite you to note down your answers to the following questions (click on https://bit.ly/DilemmaFreeGifts to access your free Manager's Problem-Solving Mindset Worksheet or just use a blank sheet of paper):

- When someone comes to you with a query, issue or problem, what is your initial response?
- What is your second response?
- Do you enjoy solving problems and resolving issues?
- How do solving problems and resolving issues make you feel?
- What value/benefit do you put on you solving problems or resolving issues?
- Do you typically extend trust to others or do they have to earn your trust?

Keep your answers somewhere safe and we will return to them in Chapter Twelve.

HOW SHOULD I BEST USE THIS BOOK?

At the end of each chapter, along with a Summary, there is a Prompts-for-You section. This section will outline some prompts as to how you can apply the chapter's content to your own team's situation. To keep your answers in one place, if you haven't done so already, please feel free to download your free Prompts-for-You Worksheet by going to https://bit.ly/DilemmaFreeGifts.

WHAT IS THE PERFORMANCE DEVELOPMENT BOOK SERIES?

The Performance Development book series is a series of books that explore the entire area of performance within business, the skills of performance development, and how to design a Performance Management and Development Process that supports strategy delivery.

This is the second book of the series. Future books will include topics such as Giving Effective Feedback, Cascading Strategic Objectives, and Reimagining Performance Management for the 21st Century.

WHY BOTHER EMPOWERING THE TEAM'S PROBLEM-SOLVING?

This is a really good question for you, as the reader, to be able to answer for yourself. As a manager, why bother to expend energy on the team's ability to problem-solve? After all, you can sort out lots of the problems anyway!

As you progress through the book, this and several related questions will be explored and answered. Chapter One: The Manager's Dilemma explores why a manager might want to think about sharing the problem-solving load. Chapter Eleven outlines a few additional benefits that can be considered the cherry on the cake. Chapter Twelve explores different mindsets that might hold a manager back from stepping into empowering their team.

In summary, all I can say is that managers who don't empower their teams end up in a lot of pain, as they struggle to manage their team and deliver the work outputs. Managers that do empower their teams tend to reap a lot of benefits within the team, within the company and in terms of their own career opportunities.

I hope that you find the book insightful and that your confidence in developing your team grows. By following this approach, trust should increase substantially. As a manager, you will be freed up while also knowing that you will be kept in the loop about any serious issues that might affect your team. Issues will be resolved and those that are escalated to you will be presented in such a way that your time will be protected while knowing that the key points have been researched and are being shared with you. You and your team will reap the performance improvements that will result.

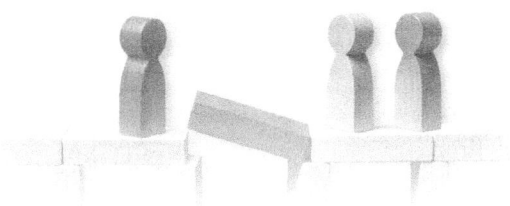

The Manager's Dilemma

What's the one "thing" that makes a good manager good?

This is a question that regularly crops up when exploring topics such as leadership, emotional intelligence, and personality styles. I customarily demur from answering the question as it's usually asked in a manner that leaves me thinking that if the questioner could just find that elusive elixir, all would be right with their world. Since there is no silver bullet to sort out all the challenges of management, I don't like to give false hope.

That said, I have noticed one "thing" being particularly prevalent in managers. It's not a "way of being" or a particular "style" of doing something. I have no formal research evidence to back up my initial observation. I can't tell you the exact percentage of the management population that demonstrates this "thing". However, I can tell you that I've run my theory past hundreds of managers and it has resonated with all of them. Of which, the most recent response was, "Yes, of course, look at how we like Gerry, because he's good at sorting stuff out while Jacob makes very little effort".

Just what is this "thing" that managers tend to be good at? In short, it's problem-solving. Managers tend to be very good at solving problems, resolving issues and getting things sorted out. To be clear, I'm not saying "every" manager is good at this. You might be thinking of Mary from accounts, who never solves problems, just leaves a trail of them behind her. Or Dan, two bosses ago, who dithered and dawdled and never seemed to make up his mind. Some managers definitely suffer from decision-making-phobia, while others are in the CYA game.

All of that said, most managers tend to be good at getting things sorted out. Why might that be? Taking a step back, who tends to get promoted? At the junior levels, the people that catch management's eye tend to be those that can figure things out, get things resolved, at least come up with some ideas and suggestions. Let's face it; people who take that approach tend to make managers' lives easier. Ironically, the employee's reward is often more work, in the guise of additional projects, high-profile projects, opportunities that provide them with greater experience, exposure and confidence. When promotional opportunities come up, who's most likely to succeed? Yep, our problem-solvers. So, they move up the ladder and into management.

Just to reiterate the point, I used to lecture third-year manufacturing-design engineering students on Human Resource Management. The module was introduced in response to evidence that showed that many engineering graduates moved into management roles within five years of graduating. What do engineers tend to be very good at? You got it, problem-solving.

Surely, managers being good at problem-solving is a good thing, right? On the face of it, yes. It would seem to be a good thing, but let's take another step back and consider it from another angle. Let's consider Trish's situation.

CASE STUDY:

Trish was delighted when she was promoted to manager and threw herself enthusiastically into her new role. Three things to know about Trish are:

1. *Trish is very good at sorting things out.*
2. *Trish has been rewarded for that, by being promoted.*
3. *Nobody sat down with Trish to explain how her job changed, what type of work she needs to focus on now, or what skills she needs to develop to succeed in her new role.*

In the absence of being told how her work has changed, and what skills she needs to succeed in the new role, Trish does her best. She has a team of six—Ericka, Lisa, Merv, Jaime, Carla and Damon—reporting in to her. From the beginning, as each and every one of them came to her with a problem, her natural instinct was to categorise it and respond in one of two ways. If it was a simple, quick answer, she told them what to do straightaway, and off they went. If it was more complex, she took it from them and sorted it out on their behalf. A few months on, Trish has found herself swamped. She decides to take some time to reflect on what is going on with the team.

Ericka is pretty good at her job and when she does come to Trish, she usually has some ideas on how to progress the issue. Ironically, Trish's concern with Ericka isn't around her ability to sort out issues, it's that she sorts them out without letting Trish know! Trish has been in a few meetings recently, with her own boss and peers, where she's been blindsided by a discussion of an issue that Ericka has sorted out. While Trish was delighted that Ericka had sorted it out, she really didn't like the feeling of helplessness she felt while sitting there, not having a clue what her peers were talking about.

At the other end of the spectrum, Merv is forever bringing issues to Trish, delightedly palming them off to her to sort out. He definitely doesn't see his role as sorting out issues! Not only that but, in their weekly team meetings, when another team member mentions any issue that he's already brought to Trish's attention, he jumps on it. He loves nothing more than to point out how he has already highlighted the issue to her. He just can't seem to let go of issues. Even when she's sorted them out, he still keeps harping on about them. Trish has noticed that every time she sees him coming near her lately, she picks up her phone and pretends to be on a call.

Trish puts Lisa somewhere between Ericka and Merv. In the tasks Lisa knows how to do, she's very good at them and Trish senses that she's well capable of doing the work and even taking on more. When Lisa does bring an issue to Trish, she's quite good at explaining what the issue is and she often has an idea or two as to how to resolve it. At times, Trish wonders why Lisa brings the issue to her at all. It seems to Trish that Lisa knows what to do, she's just too afraid to do it without Trish's permission.

Jaime just wants to know what to do and get on with it. Once Trish tells him what to do, he's gone again. While it's short and sweet, it's very, very regular. Jaime might interrupt her two or three times in a morning. Another thing she has noticed is that quite often he brings the same issues to her.

Trish is at a bit of a loss with Carla. Carla doesn't bring that many issues to Trish and usually, when she does, they are things that really do need to be teased out with someone else. What Trish has noticed is that, having agreed on the best course of action, Carla sometimes goes off on a solo-run and does something else instead. Trish doesn't know how often this occurs, but she is aware of at least two instances where this has definitely happened. Worse, she found out because the solutions Carla did implement caused more problems down the way, which were then brought to Trish's attention.

Finally, when Damon brings an issue to Trish, his modus operandi is to tell her the issue and then offer what he thinks is the right solution. As Trish gets into researching the issue, what she has noticed is that Damon often suggests a solution that misses the point or solves a different issue. This worries Trish quite a bit. It's like he looks out the window and sees that it's raining and, in an effort to ensure they don't get soaked, suggests that they wear wellington boots. His proffered solution is connected to the issue (the fact that it's raining), but it sort of misses the point (how do we keep ourselves dry overall rather than just our feet?).

As a new manager, Trish isn't exactly sure how her role has changed or what she is supposed to do differently. In her company and function, the processes are well-defined and there's always a pile of work to get through. She really wants to do a good job as a manager, both for herself and the team. She has found herself in the habit of sorting out problems and issues that the team brings to her because it seems the obvious thing to do. Looking around, it's what she sees other managers doing too.

Trish is swamped while her team doesn't seem to be overly stretched. She doesn't know what to do differently but strongly suspects that the current situation can't continue indefinitely.

CASE STUDY DEBRIEF

I'd love to say that Trish's situation is a one-off, but I've met way too many "Trishs" to know it's a common pattern across many industries. Before we dissect the dynamics of this case study, it would be worth your while taking a couple of minutes and reflecting on what you think is going on.

TRISH'S PERSPECTIVE OF THE DYNAMIC

As humans, we tend to continue doing what works for us. Trish was good at her job because she was good at sorting things out, i.e. problem-solving. Trish was rewarded for being good at her job, by being promoted. Consciously or unconsciously, she has clocked that she is good at her job because she sorts out problems and she gets rewarded for being good at her job, by being promoted. Trish has connected the two and concluded that she should continue doing what got her promoted, i.e. solving problems. It's also what she sees her peers and her own manager doing. When she goes to her boss, he tends to just sort it out for her or gives her direction on how best to deal with it.

In addition to her strength of problem-solving, nobody has sat down with Trish to explain the purpose of the manager role, how it differs from the functional work of the team, how her mindset needs to shift or what additional skills she needs to start developing. Her new boss just told her that her job was to ensure the team's work was completed on time. She's doing this as best she can, with the skills, experience, direction and training she has (or hasn't) been given.

TEAM'S PERCEPTION OF TRISH AND THE DYNAMIC

As for the team, Damon likes to understand the reason why one course of action might be better than another course. If he just needs a decision, he's happy to take Trish's direction. However, if there are several options, he likes to be able to have a discussion about them and work out which is the right option to take. He has noticed that this doesn't seem to be in Trish's repertoire. He can deal with that, but what he finds really irritating is when he brings an issue to her that he has sorted out, she immediately jumps in to either tell him what to do or takes it from him to sort out. She doesn't even allow him get to the end of his explanation before she's whipped it from him. He has gotten to the point where he doesn't even try anymore.

For Ericka, on the whole, she has found that Trish's direction is usually similar to what she was thinking herself, so it works as a good sense-check for her. At this stage, she's happy to just push on and sort things out herself. Since Trish often seems so busy with other stuff, Ericka doesn't want to bother her.

The first time Merv brought an issue to Trish, she took it from him and said she would sort it out. He couldn't believe his luck—off his plate and onto hers in one fell swoop! He tested it out a few times and she regularly either tells him what to do or takes it from him. It's much faster just going to Trish and getting an answer or, even better, having it taken off him than trying to figure it out himself. He's powering through his work while throwing the harder bits onto Trish's desk.

Lisa, on the other hand, really wants to learn her role and the various tasks she's responsible for. She really likes Trish and feels comfortable going to her with queries. Trish doesn't seem to mind how many times Lisa brings issues to her. She just either tells Lisa what she should do next or sorts it out for her and Lisa is happy to take the direction.

When Carla is *really* stuck, she'll bring it to Trish to discuss what the best thing to do is. Carla is a bit of a chatterbox and so sometimes she finds herself discussing her issue with others on the way back to her desk. Carla sometimes changes the final solution, off the back of these chats.

Jaime is very focused on the task. He's a do-it-and-get-it-done kinda guy. If he's stuck, he gets impatient and just goes straight to Trish to get the answer.

As is often the case when more than one person is involved, Trish's perspective is somewhat different to her team members' perspectives of the situation.

DYNAMIC SUMMARY

Ironically, the very skill that got Trish promoted is the very skill that is holding her back from being effective in her role. Without meaning to or without understanding how, she is causing unhelpful patterns of behaviour within the team. It's unwittingly starting to foment a lot of performance issues. Worse still, she's the one who is most likely to pay the highest price.

Trish is getting seriously swamped, but, all told, it's easy for her to assume that this is how she should best deal with issues that are being escalated up to her. Over several months, her approach has influenced and cemented the team's pattern of behaviour. Trish isn't finding any of it beneficial to her, her team, her boss, the business, or the clients. Nobody is really winning here, but Trish doesn't know what to do differently.

THE MANAGER'S DILEMMA

Trish's issue is the same one that many managers face. They are good at problem-solving. They get promoted into management because they are good at problem-solving. They have tangible evidence that being good at problem-solving is a skill that is valued and rewarded. They have likely internalised that their value to the company, and by extension to their career, lies in their ability to solve problems and sort things out. What do people do when they have been rewarded? They continue to demonstrate the behaviours that earned them the reward, i.e. they continue to sort out issues and solve problems. For most managers, this belief is happening in the subconscious, rather than something they are consciously aware of.

As their team starts to naturally escalate issues and problems to them, the manager naturally starts solving those problems too. The team members, whether they mean to or not, often fall in line and start escalating more and more issues to them. The manager starts to get swamped with too many issues being escalated, but it's a little too late and they don't know how to break the pattern.

In an effort to juggle all the balls, they might push out, or stop doing, some of their own, higher-value work to buy time to sort through the team's issues. The learnt helplessness of the team can result in decision fatigue for the manager. In turn, the manager may start escalating issues up to their own manager, particularly if they see a similar pattern of behaviour with their own manager.

The alternative is to stop taking on the team's problems and help them to develop their abilities to sort out most of their own issues. However, in a lot of organisations there's no proof that being good at developing and empowering the team will be rewarded. In these cultures, a leap of faith is needed.

The manager's dilemma boils down to:

Do I stop doing what I have been rewarded for, i.e. solving problems myself, or do I invest my time and effort into learning the additional skills that will allow me to develop my team members' problem-solving skills and empower the team to solve their own issues?

The crux of the manager's dilemma becomes: will the skill of empowering my team's problem-solving be as valued and rewarding as the proven rewards associated with my ability to solve problems?

ORGANISATIONAL IMPLICATIONS OF THE MANAGER'S DILEMMA

What happens if we extrapolate this dynamic further up the organisational levels? Either Trish's manager spots the dynamic and coaches Trish on how to break the cycle or, more likely, Trish looks to her own manager and sees that this is what he does with his own team, i.e. with Trish and her peers. In the absence of any other ideas on how to deal with it, she naturally imitates him. It is likely that this goes right up through the function or department. It may even spread out across other functions and be imbued within the organisation's culture. This is, after all, how cultures become entrenched.

For organisations in this space, they now have a wider problem with work being inappropriately escalated up to more senior, and more costly, roles. All of a sudden, a task or process that is designed to take two hours, at a cost of $20 per hour, is being half delivered by employees at the appropriate level and half delivered by someone whose position attracts a cost of $35 per hour. To put it another way, a $40 task is now costing the organisation $55, a cost increase of 37.5%.

Multiply that pattern out across several tasks and, all of a sudden, the cost base is way out of kilter with the price of the product or service. Needless to say, there's no bumping the price by 37.5% to offset the unnecessary increase in cost. This doesn't even factor in the opportunity costs of the work that the more senior person should be, but isn't, getting done due to this dynamic. Things such as: client service, business development, process improvement, communication, developing capabilities, etc.

If that's food for thought, and a little scary to think too deeply about, on the bright side, you're reading the right book. We will explore what really drives escalation and what valid and invalid reasons for escalation look like. Using Trish and her team, we will explore the mindset of the manager, along with several potential team member mindsets, and how these can feed into the unhelpful dynamics that can become established. Most importantly of all, we will explore how to diagnose a team member's possible problem-solving starting point. We will use the SMART framework as the basis of understanding where to start coaching each team member so that they get to the point of only escalating valid issues and are clear on their reason(s) for escalating. For escalated issues, we will explore how a manager can coach a team member through the various stages of problem-solving so that they become confident in sorting out most of the typical issues that arise within their role. Finally, we'll explore how best to introduce the new approach within your team and how to embed it into your team's ways of working.

SUMMARY

Many managers are promoted as a reward for being able to sort out issues and problems, i.e. they are rewarded for their problem-solving. As humans, a natural response is to continue doing what we got rewarded for in the past, in this case problem-solving.

The manager's dilemma boils down to: will the skill of empowering my team's problem-solving be as valued and rewarding as the proven rewards associated with my ability to solve problems?

The cost of deciding to continue sorting out all the issues is that the team becomes disempowered and the manager becomes overwhelmed. That said, many managers plough on, working longer hours, and do earn several more promotions. However, as per the Peter Principle, they will eventually be promoted to their own level of incompetence. They also pay a high personal price of long hours, missed life experiences and burnout.

Investing the time and effort to empower the team does take energy upfront. It may even take some longer days to give individual team members sufficient time while also delivering other work. However, this time and effort is investing in changing the future, both the manager's and the individual's. Over time, the individual will be better able to sort out their own issues, only the really important points will be escalated and, as we will see in Chapter Two, the escalation will be done in a much more effective and time-saving manner.

Some managers take the gamble while many don't even recognise the dilemma. Unwittingly, they end up continuing to sort out many of the team's issues and creating a dynamic that holds back performance—the individual's, the team's, the manager's, the organisation's. While there are many aspects to it, some key contributors to generating this unhelpful dynamic rest on the manager's own drivers, habits and lack of awareness of how to break the dynamic.

This book will explore the various aspects of (a) how to diagnose the sources of the dynamic with any individual; (b) how to design a SMART Objective that will develop and coach the individual, from the individual's likely starting point; (c) what are the acceptable valid reasons for escalation; and (d) how to introduce and embed the new approach.

PROMPTS FOR YOU

Select two to three team members and, for each of them, describe the types of behaviour you see them exhibit in relation to (1) problem-solving and (2) escalating issues. Consider what you think they *should* be able to do in this area.

If you haven't already done this for yourself, consider how sorting out issues and solving problems makes you feel. Make a note of those feelings and keep them somewhere safe.

If you haven't already done so, feel free to download the free Prompts-for-You Worksheet gift at https://bit.ly/DilemmaFreeGifts.

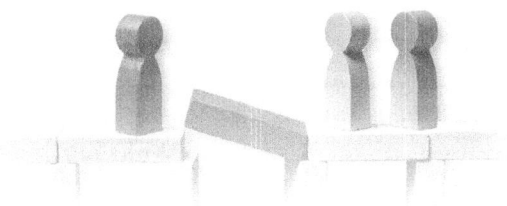

C H A P T E R   2

The Three Amigos of Escalation

What are the three valid reasons people escalate issues?

As an executive coach, I love to ask questions and this is a question I often pose when coaching or delivering the Developing Other People's Problem-Solving Skills workshop. A flavour of the most common responses includes:

- They don't know what they're doing
- They couldn't be bothered
- They're lazy
- They're looking for help
- They're lacking confidence
- They want me to sort it out for them
- They're not sure what to do
- They need me to help them make the final decision
- They know I want to see it

There's usually a slew of responses. Upon analysis, about 90% of them are similar to the sentiments expressed above. Upon further analysis, all of the above tend to fall into two broad categories; either they are invalid reasons to escalate ("they want me to sort it out for them" being a prime example) or they fall into the valid category of needing help or "a sounding board".

It's incredible how many reasons a group can throw onto the table when answering this question. As the vast majority of their responses are lobbed into either the "Invalid Reasons" category (let's call it "Needless Escalation") or "Sounding Board" category, they start wondering what the other two valid reasons for escalation could possibly be.

Some groups successfully identify the second broad category, i.e. it is being escalated because it is a true escalation. What do we mean by "true escalation"? It refers to situations whereby the team member in their role, with its related authority and power, has done everything they can to get the issue resolved; however, for whatever reasons, it still hasn't been sufficiently resolved. The team member is now escalating it to their manager and asking them, in the manager's capacity with its enhanced level of authority and power, to deal with it as is appropriate.

The third broad category is never identified, unless there is enough time to ask sufficient questions to prompt the group's thinking in the right direction. That can tell you how subtle this category is. When I share this with you, you'll likely react by saying, "It isn't even a proper category". Before you do that, though, please hear me out.

The third category that I've identified is "Keeping the Manager in the Loop". "What?" I can hear you say. "How could a reason for escalating an issue be 'keeping me in the loop'"? I'd have been right there with you, but let me share with you the story of how this one dawned on me. Going back to my colleague from the Introduction, let's call her Nancy, here's how a series of conversations went over the course of several days:

CONVERSATION ONE:

Nancy: The Transfer Agency team had five people signed up to go to the Key Players course but they've just emailed to say that they can only release three people.

Me: Right, do we have a waiting list?

Nancy: No.

Me: Okay, well, send an email out to all the managers and see if they have anyone they want to send on the course.

Nancy: Okay!

CONVERSATION TWO, A FEW DAYS LATER:

Nancy: The hedge fund team is wondering if we can schedule the Futures course next month, as they've had a few new starts.

Me: What's your schedule like? Do you think you can slot an additional day in?

Nancy: Yeah, it shouldn't be any problem.

Me: Okay, well, let's do it then.

CONVERSATION THREE, NEXT DAY:

Nancy: Chris was wondering if he could have two graduates from the Induction course.

Me: Have they been allocated yet?

Nancy: No.

Me: Well, talk to HR and see if they have made any final decisions yet.

Nancy: Humph.
[Imagine the most passive aggressive sound you can and you're on the right track]

Well, that made me sit up. I had absolutely no idea how our short interaction could possibly have engendered *that* sort of response.

Me: Eh, is there something wrong?

Nancy: Yes, there *is*! I know what to do, but you keep trying to sort it out for me and tell me what to do!

Me: What? But you've been coming to me and telling me what the issues are. I thought you were coming to me for help!

Nancy: No, I was coming to tell you what the issue was and what I had done to sort it out.

And there it was, folks! She wasn't coming to me with an issue to be resolved. She was coming to me to "keep me in the loop" and, clearly, getting extremely frustrated with me constantly telling her what to do *when she knew* what to do.

Examining the structure of our conversations reveals the subtlety of this dynamic. Nancy introduced her issues as if they needed to be resolved, i.e. her first port of call was to present the issue. In no way did she indicate that she was keeping me in the loop or that she had a good sense of how to deal with the issue or, indeed, that she had already sorted it out.

Keeping in mind that the vast majority of managers tend to be good problem-solvers, what did I do? I naturally started to solve the problem and tell her what to do. It's not an unreasonable assumption that if someone is presenting a problem to you, it must mean they are looking for help.

Over time, this interplay was clearly starting to irritate Nancy, to the point that it led to the eruption. Let's be honest, I certainly didn't want to be irritating her *that* much. In addition, if I could stop her from coming to me with needless issues that she already knew how to deal with, I was all for that.

OUR LEARNINGS

Taking a deep breath, we talked through how we had managed to get to this point. As we talked through how each of us was seeing the interaction, what became apparent was:

- If you signpost the start of a conversation as "an issue or problem", you are signposting to the other person that you need help and they will kick into "action mode", i.e. they start thinking, *What is it? What needs to be done? How can I help?*

- If you signpost the start of a conversation as, "Everything is sorted, I'm just letting you know", you are signposting to the other person that they don't need to worry about anything. In turn, they recognise that all they need to do is sit back and listen.

Nancy realised that the way she initially framed the conversation was the very thing that was triggering the response in me that was driving her nuts. I realised that sometimes people don't frame their intentions or needs very clearly. This is why many managers in the USA use the question "What's the ask?" when someone comes to them with a point. While we'll see that this is a great first step, it might not go far enough to actively develop someone's ability to problem-solve, depending on where their starting point is.

While I don't usually share this story as to how I came to recognise the above dynamic, when I explain what I mean by "keeping them in the loop", managers typically nod their heads in agreement. Either they are thinking about how they present things to their own manager or they are reflecting on how one of their team might unwittingly do this. Either way, the point seems to resonate with them as valid.

Some people are naturally better at keeping others in the loop and framing it in that way. For example, they might start off their point with, "I just wanted to let you know that…" Phrasing the opening in this way signals to the manager that an issue has likely been taken care of. People who do this should be encouraged to continue, as it is good practice. For our purposes, we're considering team members that escalate by starting off with an explanation of the problem without giving any indication that they have sorted it out, as Nancy was doing.

By this stage of the workshop, we have concluded that there are three broad categories of valid reasons to escalate issues and a lot of invalid reasons that result in the dynamic of lots of issues and problems being regularly escalated. We have also concluded that there are lots of reasons that drive people to regularly escalate invalid issues and clicking our fingers isn't going to change that reality. This is a great segue into what we need to know and do to change the dynamic and substantially reduce those needless escalations.

SUMMARY

There are three broad valid reasons to escalate issues:

- – A true escalation
- – Sounding board/ genuinely needing help
- – Keeping a person in the loop

These are the three amigos of escalation. All other reasons fall into the needless escalation category and the reasons behind them occurring need to be addressed.

PROMPTS FOR YOU

Reflect on the types of issues or problems each of your team members escalate to you. For each person, identify whether their escalations typically fall into the valid or invalid reasons for escalation. If they fall into the valid categories, identify which specific category.

C H A P T E R   3

The Steps of Problem-Solving

How many steps do you think there are in the problem-solving process?

Two, three, five? Would you believe that there are actually eight steps to the problem-solving process? Managers regularly gulp when I suggest that. If you're one of the people who said, "Two", i.e. identify the problem and solve it, you're not alone. For people who are good at problem-solving (as a manager, that's highly likely to be you), solving problems is so second nature to them that they don't even recognise the steps they go through.

In this chapter, we're going to define and explore what is meant by each of these steps. Once we do a whistle-stop tour of the SMART framework, this collective understanding will then form the basis of diagnosing and designing a generic problem-solving objective in Chapters Five and Six. In Chapters Seven to Ten, we'll coach Trish through the process of diagnosing the potential starting point for each of her team members and how she might design an effective development objective for each of them.

THE EIGHT STEPS OF PROBLEM-SOLVING

Broadly speaking, the eight steps of problem-solving are:

Step One: Identify and recognise the problem
Step Two: Evaluate the size of the problem
Step Three: Research the causes of the problem
Step Four: Identify potential options
Step Five: Evaluate potential options
Step Six: Decide on the best solution
Step Seven: Implement the best solution
Step Eight: Review the outcomes

STEP ONE: IDENTIFY AND RECOGNISE THE PROBLEM

As obvious as this step seems, I include it as some people just don't recognise or identify problems. It is not for me to reflect on why this might be, nor is it within the scope of this book. It's enough to recognise that occasionally you may come across someone who falls at this hurdle. If so, it is very likely to be part of a much broader performance issue and should be addressed in that manner. For our purposes, we are going to assume that we are considering team members that are able to, at least, identify and recognise that a problem has arisen.

STEP TWO: EVALUATE THE SIZE OF THE PROBLEM

When identifying the eight steps, as part of a workshop, this is the step that is usually missed. It seems so obvious and yet its importance is regularly disregarded. From experience, people tend to fall into two categories: those that problem-identify and those that problem-solve. There is a large cohort of people who think that it is enough to just endlessly identify problems without making any effort to actually seek out or suggest solutions. Problem-identifiers tend to be very good at sniffing out issues and letting others know all about them. They can even get quite energised by identifying problems. In addition to not identifying solutions, they also tend to present every problem they identify as the same size. An issue that might impact three people will be presented with the same fervour as an issue that might impact a hundred. Take Mike for example.

Case Study

Mike excelled at identifying problems. He was a subject matter expert (SME) working as part of a project team that was responsible for implementing a new accounting system. As the project change manager, Kate had been asked to facilitate cross-functional workshops to collectively map out the processes needed to support the new system. As they mapped out and discussed one particular process, Mike said they wouldn't be able to use the reports from the new system because it might not pick up if a specific event occurred. He was a brilliant problem-identifier!

Kate took a deep breath. Mike was a core part of the project implementation team while other attendees were participating in the workshop, with the expectation that they would be using the system at some point in the coming year. If a project member was saying that the system wouldn't meet their reporting needs, Kate was aware that the other attendees could also start talking negatively about the system and cause huge problems for the implementation.

Since Kate had over ten years' experience of working with the new system and had never come across the issue Mike had raised; she decided to accept that Mike might have a valid point and asked him if he had ever seen this issue arise before. He acknowledged that he hadn't. She then asked him how likely it was that the issue would arise. They ended up agreeing that it was highly unlikely to arise. Kate summarised by acknowledging that while it was a possibility that the issue could arise, the probability of it actually arising was so negligible that they could safely set it aside and move on.

CASE STUDY DEBRIEF

As a problem-identifier, as far as Mike was concerned, his job was done once he had identified the vaguest possibility of an issue and it was up to Kate to deal with it. What he didn't recognise was that highlighting something without acknowledging the likely size of the potential impact wasn't doing his reputation any good. When his issue was exposed as being sufficiently improbable that it could safely be ignored, there was then a question mark over his ability to frame the issue in a manner that allowed the concern to be raised while recognising that it was unlikely to happen.

If you have come across a problem-identifier, you'll know how tiring it is to deal with them. They often highlight issues that are non-issues and won't let them go. They often have a tendency to keep bringing the issue up, even after decisions have been made. There are several reasons behind why they might behave in this way. However, this book is focused on how to highlight to them the need to incorporate this step into their overall approach to problem-solving rather than to expend energy on trying to figure out what those reasons might be.

Identifying the size of the problem has a huge bearing on the next step. If it is determined that the impact of the problem is negligible, then the issue can be categorised as a non-issue and there's no need to progress further, recognising that while it has the potential to become an issue, the unlikely probability of it being an immediate issue allows it to be set aside for the moment. If it is determined that the impact is sizeable enough, then it will need to be dealt with, which nicely moves us to step three.

By the end of step two, a person should be able to say why an issue is large enough that it's worth the time and energy to sort it out. They need to be able to explain "why this matters", if you will. Evaluating the size of the problem might also need to include the knock-on impacts of it, e.g. who or what will be impacted by this?

For example, a report that doesn't include a particular data column may not be much of an issue for the IT report-development team. For the sales team, not having access to that data column means they can't tell at what point in the sales process they lose potential clients, so they can't pinpoint where they need to improve their sales process. Lost sales results in less revenue within the business, which has numerous knock-on effects for everyone within the organisation, both in terms of budgets and investing in the business and its people. To summarise, while the issue of the missing data column isn't going to have a major impact on the IT report-development team, it will create all sorts of issues and a need for workarounds for the sales team.

Another example might be changing the organisational policy around employee car parking. Such a policy change might impact three people or a hundred and three people. In addition, it might depend which specific people make up those numbers. The hundred and three people may all be people who don't drive to work anyway so aren't that bothered by a change in the car parking policy. For the three that are being impacted, it could include someone with such specific parking needs that it's going to have a very material impact on them.

To recap, determining the size of an issue provides a decision point. It determines whether it is appropriate to put additional time and effort into resolving the issue or whether it can be acknowledged and either deemed negligible or insufficiently important at the current time. Skipping this step can result in wasting effort and time on resolving issues that aren't of merit.

STEP THREE: RESEARCH THE CAUSE(S) OF THE PROBLEM

For our purposes, this step is around ensuring that all the drivers of the cause of the problem are identified and their impacts are understood. Depending on the type of issue, "research" could just mean taking five minutes reflecting on what might have happened to have caused the issue. It could mean asking a few questions and confirming the answers. It could also mean in-depth running reports, applying research techniques, talking to people, physically examining a machine, etc. In short, "research" means whatever ways are appropriate to get to the bottom of what is causing the problem.

As mentioned in the Introduction, this book doesn't cover out specific tools and techniques of how to research, diagnose or evaluate the best solution. It assumes that, as a manager, you already know how to use and apply the tools as appropriate for your industry, company, function and typical issues. For example, in Manufacturing and Engineering, the Fishbone technique is a very common diagnostic tool, used to get to the root causes of the issue. On the other hand, in Advertising and Marketing, they might rely heavily on market research to help them research the causes of their challenge.

A very common trait of company culture is a tendency towards identifying the sticking-plaster solution, to cover over the cracks, rather than a preventative solution i.e., one that prevents it from re-occurring. So, regardless of the approach taken to research the issue, it is important to get to the root causes of it. There is much literature on the importance of determining root cause analysis and how to do it, so we're not going to get into it in any depth here. However, when we get to the later stages of problem-solving, it will become important to understand the difference between an immediate short-term solution and a longer-term fix.

In a multitude of fast-paced industries, the need for an immediate resolution is sometimes paramount, so the "sticking plaster" fix becomes the norm. If it's a one-off issue, this shouldn't be an issue, assuming the sticking plaster solution doesn't cause any knock-on problems. However, some issues are actually recurring ones. Understanding the reasons for the issue in the first place helps us in two ways. Firstly, it helps us to categorise it into either one-off or recurring. Secondly, for recurring issues, understanding the drivers that cause the recurrence allows us to incorporate a longer-term aspect into the solution.

As we will see later, encouraging team members to research the causes of the issue will enable them to categorise it and determine if they need a longer-term fix alongside an immediate one. Building a habit of implementing longer-term fixes can very quickly free up teams from doing tasks that absorb a lot of needless effort on an on-going basis.

For example, a five minute "quick" workaround that a team of five has to do twice a day equates to fifty minutes per day. Over a year, that equates to 215 hours or over twenty-seven days. Not so "quick" when put in those terms. On the other hand, taking two hours to design and implement a long-term solution, providing a thirty-minute training session to the other team members, and then monitoring implementation over a week, equating to roughly two hours, comes to the grand total of four and half hours, or just over a half a day.

STEP FOUR: IDENTIFY POTENTIAL OPTIONS

If steps three [research the causes], five [evaluate options] and six [decide on the best solution] draw heavily on the skill of analysis, step four draws on the skill of creativity. When identifying potential options, there are always the obvious ones, particularly in relation to the quick-fix solutions. However, given the continuous amount of change organisations face, how quickly technology goes out of date, the potential impact on people and how they may react, the obvious options aren't necessarily the best choices. For organisations that state a value somewhere in the Innovation arena, the obvious options really aren't (or shouldn't, if they're serious about Innovation and Creativity) going to cut it.

So, along with identifying the obvious options, this step is also about pushing ourselves to identify the not-so-obvious options. The deeper the causes of the issue are understood from step three the easier it is to identify options beyond the visible.

Depending on the issue, its size and impact, whether it's a one-off or recurring, etc., the ideal number of potential options will vary. For a one-off smallish issue that isn't going to be particularly controversial, generating two or three options may be sufficient. For a controversial issue that is likely to be noticed and has the potential to cause reactions, generating five or six options might be prudent to ensure a broad enough range is considered. Again, the better the understanding of the impact(s) of the issue the more options are likely to be identified.

Another interesting point about identifying potential options is that it also includes naming ones that are likely to be considered non-starters. The purpose of this step is to identify possible options, not to evaluate them. Combining the identification and evaluation into one step stunts creativity and our ability to find the best solution. So even if a potential option is likely to be dismissed straightaway in step five [evaluation], it is still worthwhile including it in this step. By doing so, it forces us to properly evaluate why it is a non-starter in step 5, rather than just assuming it isn't a valid option. It broadens thinking, thus increasing creativity.

Ultimately, as a rule of thumb, the more options that are generated the better the final solution will be. In executive coaching, coaches sometimes use a technique called the Rule of +2. Once a coachee thinks they have exhausted all their options, the coach challenges them to come up with another two ideas (plus two). Some really creative options have come out of using this technique. In certain circumstances, it might be a useful tool for you, as the manager, to use, particularly with someone who doesn't appear to be trying very hard.

STEP FIVE: EVALUATE POTENTIAL OPTIONS

Once a sufficient number of options have been generated, the next step is to sift through and evaluate them. During this step, each identified option needs to be evaluated and assessed against whether or not it meets at least the following criteria:

- – Resolves the immediate needs of the issue
- – Resolves the longer-term needs of the issue

- Ease of implementation
- Knock-on impacts
- Whether it is within or outside sphere of control
- If outside sphere of control, the likelihood of those impacted agreeing
- Effort/cost vs. return
- Risks
- Applicable regulatory requirements

Since different industries and functions have different needs and concerns, this is by no means an exhaustive list. In addition, as a manager, you'll have your own list of criteria that serves you well in your own context. Please feel free to adjust and add additional criteria that you have identified, as relevant to your particular environment.

Once evaluated, each option can be categorised to whittle it down to a shortlist of final options. Again, while not an exhaustive list, such categories could include:

- Non-starters
- Immediate vs. long-term
- Within own control
- Needs input/approval from others
- Possibilities
- Likely options
- More information needed

Working through this step helps us to form the basis of the final decision, which takes place as part of the next step. As you are reading this, you might be thinking, *I don't have time to do all that!* In reality, you probably work through a similar list in your head but you do it so quickly that you don't even notice. Next time you're sorting out an issue, slow down and jot down all the elements you evaluate potential options against and then how you categorise and whittle down the options to get to a final solution. This is what you need to be able to articulate and coach your team towards.

For options that fall into categories such as "Needs Input/Approval from Others" or "More Information Needed", part of this step would include the whole process of discussing and exploring the issue sufficiently to allow full sight of the feasibility of that option and what the potential solution might look like.

Depending on the type, size and complexity of the issue, this evaluation step can run the gamut from "not even registering as a distinct step" to "requiring several iterations" before a final shortlist of options is compiled.

STEP SIX: DECIDE ON THE BEST SOLUTION

Step six is where the actual decision is made. This is a discrete step in itself but for some managers, it might seem like it happens as one big massive step, consisting of steps 4, 5 and 6.

Diverse industries, functions and organisations have different ways to make the actual decision. Managers might also bring their own nuances to the process. Again, this book isn't going to get into the various tools and techniques that can be used to come to a decision. The assumption is that, as a manager, you have an appropriate understanding of what will fly in your own organisation and it is on that basis that you will be developing your own team members' abilities to effectively conclude this step.

What this step does include, regardless of industry or organisational considerations, is the process of mixing and matching some of the options to create an overall solution. For example, the final decision might comprise immediate and longer-term elements arising from combining aspects of several different discrete options. Or the solution might include tasks that address both the process that will be used along with socialising the idea with stakeholders to gain buy-in or prevent kick-back.

In Chapters Nine and Twelve, we will explore some of the human dynamics that might hold a person back from actually making a decision.

STEP SEVEN: IMPLEMENT THE BEST SOLUTION

This step is fairly straightforward and revolves around implementing the decision. For many managers, this step isn't where their concerns and frustrations arise. Usually, they find that once they tell the person what to do to resolve the issue, the person goes on their merry way and sorts it out. However, situations have arisen whereby the best solution has been agreed and then, for whatever reason, changes have been made to what actually is implemented. If this scenario invokes an image of someone you know, as an added bonus we'll explore what might be causing this pattern of behaviour in Chapter Ten.

STEP EIGHT: REVIEW THE OUTCOMES

If step two [evaluate the size of the problem] wins the award for Least Likely to Be Identified, this step wins the award for Most Forgotten, and that goes for both team members and managers. The usual response to this is, "Oh yeah, of course!" It goes without saying that this should be included but, given the busyness of the world, it is usually forgotten about. However, it's a good habit to get into and is particularly helpful as a change management tool.

Reviewing the outcomes can be as informal as taking five minutes to reflect on the answers to questions such as: Has that issue been sorted? Is it working? Has it caused any other issues? As with many projects, this step could be formally captured as a task, such as preparing a note or updating a report on the issue, noting what was the solution, the outcomes and the learnings. Another option could be to ask a team member to prepare and deliver a short presentation to the rest of the team so that everyone learns.

Taking the time to complete step eight has several benefits. Firstly, it embeds the learning. Secondly, it allows team members to recognise their achievements and the progress made. Thirdly, it builds team members' confidence in their analysis and decision-making. Lastly, it positively affirms the process, further reinforcing the embedding of the process in the team's ways of working.

PROBLEM-SOLVING STEPS CHALLENGES

As mentioned at the start of this chapter, the process of working through the above eight steps has become second nature to most managers. For many, they're not even aware that they work through some of the steps. In workshops, while participants can recognise the broad thrust of each of the eight steps, they often mix in the activities of several steps into one overall step. As we work through Chapters Five through Ten, we now have a shared understanding of what each step encompasses.

Coupled with the manager's own challenges in having a clear understanding of the problem-solving steps, they also need to figure out which specific step(s) a team member might be struggling with and then decide how they will approach developing and coaching that individual. The manager could have two or three different team members struggling with different steps.

Before jumping into diagnosing where individual team members' starting points might be, we'll have a quick look at the SMART objective setting process in the next chapter. If you have already read my *SMART Objective Setting for Managers* book, feel free to go straight to Chapter Five. If you haven't read the book or you want a quick recap, I recommend that you go to Chapter Four to ensure your understanding of SMART matches my approach to using SMART, which we will be using in Chapters Six through Ten.

SUMMARY

There are eight steps to effective problem-solving:

1. Identifying and recognising the problem
2. Evaluating the size of the problem
3. Researching the causes of the problem
4. Identifying potential options
5. Evaluating potential options
6. Deciding on the best solution
7. Implementing the best solution
8. Reviewing the outcomes

PROMPTS FOR YOU

As you read through the list of eight steps, use them to reflect on your own process of problem-solving. Identify aspects that are of particular importance that you take into consideration, given your industry, organisation, function. These could be aspects such as: political, financial, brand reputation, the general public or relational.

If you don't already have a clear list of criteria you use for evaluating (step five) and deciding (step six), take some time to reflect on, and note down, the criteria you instinctively use.

C H A P T E R   4

The SMART Model Overview

For those of you who haven't read *SMART Objective Setting for Managers*, this chapter is a whistle-stop tour of the key points of using the SMART model. If you have read the book, you're more than welcome to read this chapter, as a reminder of the key points, or feel free to move straight to Chapter Five: Diagnosing the Starting Point.

If you're still reading this chapter, let's have a quick recap of what SMART stands for and then we'll go into the key points to be aware of before we dive into Chapter Five. SMART is an acronym for:

S—Specific:	Describes, in detail, a goal to be achieved
M—Measurable:	Explains how successful achievement of this goal will be measured
A—Attainable:	Considers whether it is possible to achieve this goal
R—Relevant or Realistic:	Explains why achieving the goal matters (relevant) or what can realistically be achieved. We will use Relevant.
T—Timeframe:	Indicates by when the goal should be achieved

The theory behind SMART is that a goal is more likely to be achieved if it is turned into a concrete target of what we want to achieve (specific) with a clear idea of what success will look like (measurement), so we can recognise it when we get there; it should include an idea of when we expect to have achieved it by (timeframe), why we want to achieve it (relevance), and finally, if we really think it is possible to achieve this (attainable) or if there are some constraints to be considered.

The whistle-stop tour of key points when using SMART as part of performance management and development, AKA using SMART as a tool of management, includes:

- The usual SMART literature assumes the person setting the goal is setting the goal for themselves. When setting a goal with another person, i.e. a team member, this assumption doesn't hold up. Thus, the communication process rears its ugly head to seriously complicate the use of SMART between two (or more) people.

- Objectives can be categorised into four broad types:
  o   Role specific
  o   Business aligned
  o   Technical developmental
  o   Behavioural developmental

- An objective may cover out two or more objective types. For example, an objective to deliver a project that is key to achieving an element of a business's strategy might be both business aligned and develop the person's technical project management skills.

- While the typical way to use Timeframe is to specify a date by which the objective should be achieved, my approach is to use this heading to outline and agree a specific plan as to how the objective will be achieved. Using Timeframe in this way helps to combat the potential communication issues that can arise.

    To ensure that both parties have a similar view of how to achieve the objective and that the plan remains on track and/or is realistic, dates and timeframes can be included against the steps of the plan. For example, if a person needs to take on a new monthly task, Timeframe might look something like this:
    o   End-month one: Attend in-house training course

o Months two to four: Learn all aspects of task via on-the-job training
o Month five onwards: Consistently complete monthly task on time and to agreed standard

- Measurement should be captured in terms of final outputs or outcomes, rather than as a task or step that needs to be completed as part of achieving the goal. For example, following on from the point above, many managers would call out "Attending training course" as the measurement of determining if this goal is achieved or not. They select it because, on initial examination, it seems like a tangible and objective way to measure success.

  If you've ever sent someone on a course, you'll know that, while they may indeed have attended the course, whether they actually incorporate the learning and do something different off the back of having attended it is a totally different kettle of fish. For an objective measured in this way, it would be very easy for the employee to argue that they have successfully achieved the objective (i.e. they attended the course) without ever having taken over the responsibility of doing the task.

  Instead, the measurement should be captured with something along the lines of: to consistently and accurately deliver this task by the last business day of the month. To recap, the agreed measurement should be captured in terms of the outcome (e.g. to take responsibility for delivering the task to the correct standards and within the appropriate timeframe) and not in terms of a step that must be done to complete the task (e.g. to attend a training course).

- As part of Attainable, it's important to consider the context within which the objective will be delivered and potential gaps, supports and constraints should be surfaced and discussed. So, while on the surface of it an objective might seem to be attainable, in reality, if certain conditions are not met, the objective may actually be unattainable. If these conditions are very obvious but are not acknowledged, the objective may be dead on arrival before you've even left the objective-setting meeting. Failure to acknowledge and discuss obvious concerns is very demotivating to the team member and is likely to result in resentment and an unachieved goal.

Following on from the example above, if the person is sent on the in-house course and then nobody is assigned to provide them the on-the-job training, how attainable is it? Or if the training course is only run twice a year and it has just been run, is it attainable?

– Relevance should link the objective to the driver(s) that is generating it. Drivers include:
   o   Role specific: person is still learning their role
   o   Strategy: objective comes directly from the business strategy
   o   Performance: a specific gap has been identified and needs to be addressed. This could be technical or behavioural

– Behavioural objectives are ones that focus on "how" a person is going about a task rather than the specific task they are doing. It tends to be considered a more personal type of objective than the other types. A good way to depersonalise it is to answer the question: *what's the business impact of this identified behaviour that needs to change?*

– When diagnosing behavioural "how" concerns, the suggested approach is to note down the observable behaviour and then ask: *what is this an example of?* It may be necessary to ask this question several times before getting to the real source of the concerns the behaviour is highlighting.

The premise of *The Manager's Dilemma* is firmly rooted in the "behavioural developmental objective" space to develop and empower your team's problem-solving abilities. The above points should provide you with a sufficient overview of the key points to be aware of, both in terms of designing SMART objectives and diagnosing behavioural drivers.

SUMMARY

SMART is a framework that permits a two-way conversation, to discuss, agree and design appropriate objectives linked back to the person's role, developmental needs or business strategy.

SMART stands for:

S   Specific
M   Measurable
A   Attainable
R   Relevance
T   Timeframe

Behavioural objectives need to be diagnosed in terms of what is really driving the observable (how) behaviours, while they should be framed (Relevance) in terms of business impact.

PROMPTS FOR YOU

In preparation for the next chapter, select a member of your team and identify a way in which they approach their role that raises concerns or red flags for you.

Try to articulate what the source of this behavioural concern is by answering the question, "What is this an example of?" several times until you get to what you suspect the source of the behaviour might be.

Then try to articulate why this behaviour is of concern by answering the question, "What is the business impact of this?" Again, you might need to ask the question several times to get to a credible answer. If you can't identify a credible business impact, consider if this is your own idiosyncrasy and reflects how you like things done rather than an actual behavioural issue.

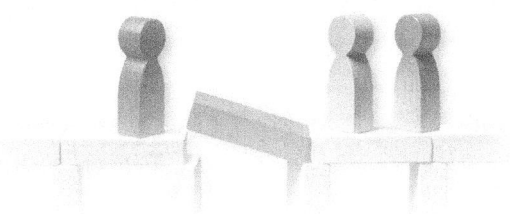

C H A P T E R 5

Diagnosing the Starting Point

In this chapter, we're going to spend some quality time with Trish and see if we can help her understand exactly what is going on with her team members. If you recall, Trish was very good at problem-solving, hence her promotion to management and her tendency to sort out the team's issues. Things have come to a head and she's recognised that she can't keep sorting out all the problems escalated up to her. She needs to completely rethink how the team operates. Successfully devolving most of the problem-solving responsibility to the team is the most feasible option she can see.

She has a team of six people reporting to her—Ericka, Lisa, Merv, Jaime, Carla and Damon. Here's a quick reminder of Trish's view of each of them.

Ericka is pretty good at her job and when she does come to Trish, she usually has some ideas on how to progress the issue. Ironically, Trish's concern with Ericka isn't around her ability to sort out issues, it's that she sorts them out without letting Trish know! Trish has been in a few meetings recently, with her own boss and peers, where she's been blindsided by a discussion of an issue that Ericka has sorted out. While Trish was delighted that Ericka had sorted it out, she really didn't like the feeling of helplessness she felt while sitting there, not having a clue what her peers were talking about.

At the other end of the spectrum, Merv is forever bringing issues to Trish, delightedly palming them off to her to sort out. He definitely doesn't see his role as sorting out issues! Not only that but, in their weekly team meetings, when another team member mentions any issues that he has already brought to Trish's attention, he jumps on it. He loves nothing more than to point out how he has already highlighted the issue to her. He just can't seem to let go of issues. Even when she's sorted them out, he still keeps harping on about them. Trish has noticed that every time she sees him coming near her lately, she picks up her phone and pretends to be on a call.

Trish would put Lisa somewhere between Ericka and Merv. In the tasks Lisa knows how to do, she's very good at them and Trish senses that she's well capable of doing the work and even taking on more. When Lisa does bring issues to Trish, she's quite good at explaining what the issue is and she often has an idea or two as to how to resolve it. At times, Trish wonders why Lisa brings the issue to her at all. It seems to Trish that Lisa knows what to do, she's just too afraid to do it without Trish's permission.

Jaime just wants to know what to do and get on with it. Once Trish tells him what to do, he's gone again. While it's short and sweet, it's very, very regular. Jaime might interrupt her two or three times in a morning. Another thing she's noticed is that quite often he brings the same issues to her.

Trish is at a bit of a loss with Carla. Carla doesn't bring that many issues to Trish and, usually, when she does, they are things that really do need to be teased out with someone else. What Trish has noticed is that, having agreed on the best course of action, Carla sometimes goes off on a solo-run and does something else instead. Trish doesn't know how often this occurs, but she knows of at least two instances where this definitely has happened. Worse, she found out because the solutions Carla implemented caused more problems down the way, which were then brought to Trish's attention.

Finally, when Damon brings an issue to Trish, his modus operandi is to tell her the issue and then offer what he thinks is the right solution. As Trish gets into researching the issue, what she has noticed is that Damon often suggests a solution that misses the point or solves a different issue. This worries Trish quite a bit. It's like he looks out the window and sees that it's raining and, in an effort to ensure they don't get soaked, suggests that they wear wellington boots. His proffered solution is connected to the issue (the fact that it's raining), but it sort of misses the point (how do we keep ourselves dry overall rather than just our feet?).

Since Trish would never be able to carve out sixty minutes of pure uninterrupted time at her desk, she has decided to block off her diary for an hour and book a meeting room. She recognises that this is the only way she is going to be able to really take the time to reflect on what is going on with her team. So,

Trish is sitting in a meeting room, door closed, a sheet of paper in front of her, with the eight steps of problem-solving and three valid reasons for escalation written out, as shown in Table 5.1: Summary of Problem-Solving Steps and Reasons for Escalation.

Table 5.1: Summary of Problem-Solving Steps and Reasons for Escalation

8 STEPS OF PROBLEM-SOLVING		3 VALID REASONS FOR ESCALATION
1	Identify and recognise problem	To keep manager in the loop
2	Evaluate the size of problem	Needs help/sounding board
3	Research the causes of problem	True escalation
4	Identify potential options	
5	Evaluate potential options	
6	Decide on best solution	
7	Implement best solution	
8	Review outcomes	

Starting with Ericka, Trish reflects on the typical types of behaviours she sees Ericka displaying and asks herself, "Is this a problem-solving or escalation issue?" Straightaway, she can see that Ericka might well be able to solve issues but she's most certainly *NOT* keeping Trish in the loop. Upon further reflection, while Ericka is good at problem-solving, Trish feels that Ericka could be a bit more thorough in her analysis and final selection and could also be a little more creative in thinking beyond the obvious. Trish places her at step four.

Moving onto Merv, Trish can see immediately that Merv is a problem-identifier and not a problem-solver. Since he never actually solves any problems, she has absolutely no idea if he's any good at it or not. First things first, though, she needs to start with getting Merv to recognise that part of his job is to actually solve problems, not *just* identify them! Trish quickly jots his name down against step two.

Having noted down the typical behaviours she sees Lisa demonstrate and asking herself the question, "What is this an example of?" Trish's answers aren't neatly falling into either the eight steps or the three valid reasons. The closest she can place them is somewhere in the "needing help/sounding board", but it's not quite that either. At this point, she feels that Lisa should be able to resolve a decent chuck of the issues she brings to her, since she often has a sense of the right thing to do. It's like Lisa doesn't believe in herself, that she's lacking confidence in herself. Trish isn't exactly sure what step "lacking confidence" falls into, but she notes it down anyway because that's what she feels the actual issue is. She decides to put Lisa's name against step six.

Trish recognises in Jaime the quintessential "needless escalator". Jaime doesn't really want to think, he just wants to "do". Trish can see that, while it might be faster for him to just get the answer and move on, it is slowing her down substantially. It's fine if she's already in problem-solving mode or if she hasn't gotten stuck into something; but when she's deeply engrossed in a task and he interrupts her, she finds it very difficult to get back into her flow. Sometimes, her concentration is so disrupted that she has to move on to another task to help her refocus. It might not bother Jaime, but it really doesn't work for her. As she thinks about it, that's definitely a business impact of this habit.

What Trish isn't so sure about is how this dynamic was created. Thinking about it, she doesn't know if this pattern arose because Jaime struggles with problem-solving or if he quickly worked out that it was easier and faster for him to just get the answer from Trish and Trish hasn't pushed back on him yet. Again, she isn't sure what step Jaime is starting from as she never sees him try to sort an issue out. She figures he is likely to be somewhere between steps two, three and five.

Taking a look at Carla, Trish recognises that she doesn't trust that Carla will carry out what they've agreed. Of late, she has found herself regularly checking in with her to ensure she has done what they have agreed. After that, she's at a loss as to *what* is going on with Carla. Why would she agree to a solution and then just go off and do something else? Whatever is going on, Carla's issue would seem to fall into step seven of problem-solving (Implementing Solution), but that's about as far as Trish can take it, for the moment, and she notes Carla's name against that step.

Last, but not least, Trish reflects on what is going on with Damon. She has a very serious question mark over Damon's analysis and logic skills and really doesn't trust that he'll make the right decision. Even though he makes an effort to try to sort out issues, he is actually the person Trish is most concerned about. It can be very hard to build up trust in another person when you have serious doubts about their ability. She notes his name down against step three.

Having reflected on where she thinks issues are arising for each person, Trish looks over her completed analysis, as shown in Table 5.2: Problem-Solving Team Analysis Summary:

Table 5.2: Problem-Solving Team Analysis Summary

	8 STEPS OF PROBLEM-SOLVING	TEAM MEMBER NAME	COMMENT
1	Identify and recognise problem		
2	Evaluate the size of problem	Merv	Focus on solving problems
3	Research the causes of problem	Damon	Improve issue diagnosis?
4	Identify potential options	Ericka	Bring in creativity?
5	Evaluate potential options		
6	Decide on best solution	Lisa	Build up confidence
7	Implement best solution	Carla	????
8	Review outcomes		

Trish isn't sure where she should place Jaime's name in the table. She just doesn't have enough evidence to put him anywhere.

As we can see from Trish's initial analysis, there are numerous points at which an individual might struggle with problem-solving. In the event of not knowing how to move to the next step of the process they escalate the issue, for the valid reason of needing help and/or a sounding board. What they found was someone (in this case, Trish) who was willing to just give them the answer or take it and sort it out. That response didn't necessarily meet their need to learn how to sort the issue out for the next time. However, it did sort the immediate need to get the issue sorted, allowing them to resume their work.

Recognising that perhaps an individual has gotten stuck somewhere along the process and needs help to become unstuck, rather than having many of their issues sorted out for them, can help the manager invest the time to try to figure out which stage of the problem-solving process the individual has gotten stuck in. Taking time out to analyse the observable behaviours and reflect on where the individual might be getting stuck provides clues as to where a person's starting point in developing their problem-solving skills might be.

While they can provide clues, they are only that—clues. As managers, we still need to support the evidence with actual dialogue that helps us and the individual pinpoint exactly where their starting point is. After all, as we saw in Chapter One: The Manager's Dilemma, they'll have their own perspective. Recalling my colleague, Nancy, I could have decided that her starting point was around identifying potential options and gotten myself into even more hot water! By having the conversation with her, we were able to identify that it was her manner of signposting the escalation rather than her ability to identify the best solution.

As Trish looks at her team analysis summary, she feels good that she has been able to put some shape on the ballpark she is starting from with each of her team members. She's desperately trying to hold on to the positive sense that she's made progress while trying to ignore the gnawing worry creeping over her—what does she do now?

As it is for many managers, it's a lot easier to articulate where a team member might be getting stuck. It's a lot harder to figure out how to design a development plan so that they can fully step into sorting out issues within their remit and only escalate issues for valid reasons. Before we coach Trish through designing potential development plans for each of her team members using the SMART framework, we will first examine a generic developmental plan in the next chapter. This will provide us with a good overview of what "good" problem-solving and escalation looks like.

SUMMARY

It's important to identify and articulate the observable behaviours a team member is exhibiting and reflect on which steps they might be struggling with. While for some team members this will be fairly obvious, for others it may be harder to pinpoint. Two very common themes that this process surfaces are "confidence" and "trust".

Reflecting on the observable behaviours of a team member and considering which of the eight problem-solving step(s) and/or the three valid reasons for escalation they appear to be grappling with provides a good starting point for designing a potential development plan for the individual.

PROMPTS FOR YOU

For each of your team members, reflect on the patterns of behaviour they exhibit and consider which step(s) they may be grappling with. Using the Prompts for You Free Gift, https://bit.ly/DilemmaFreeGifts, or using a blank sheet of paper, note down which step(s), valid escalation issue(s) and/or theme(s) you think could be tripping them up.

C H A P T E R S I X

Designing a Generic Problem-Solving Objective

In this chapter, we're going to focus on using SMART to design a generic problem-solving developmental objective, starting from step two of problem-solving. In the following three chapters, we will then apply that understanding specifically to Trish's team and demonstrate how it works for five of her six team members. Since Carla's issue is likely to be pulling from a totally different source, but is still causing headaches for Trish and her team's ability to consistently execute effective problem-solving, we will examine what might be causing that unusual dynamic separately, in Chapter Ten.

As mentioned in Chapter Three, we have assumed that each team member is able to recognise when an issue arises or needs to be dealt with. On that basis, we will start from Step Two: Evaluating the Size of the Problem. Let's start crafting a SMART objective that actively develops a person's ability to solve problems.

SPECIFIC

Starting with Specific, what exactly is the objective that Trish needs to design? What would need to happen for the individual to be successful at resolving the common issues they encounter? For issues that really do need to be escalated, how should they be presented to ensure maximum value from Trish's input while minimising the time required of her? You might want to compile your own additional points, but for most managers, at a minimum, the specific objective is likely to include the following:

- Consistently and effectively solve the majority of issues that fall within individual's role.
- When escalating an issue, clearly signpost the reason for escalation, i.e.:
  o Keeping them in the loop
  o Need help/sounding board
  o A true escalation
- When escalating a "needs help/sounding board" issue, at a minimum, they need to be able to explain:
  o What the issue is and why it's an issue (Steps One and Two: Identify the Issue and Size)
  o What is causing the issue (Step Three: Research Causes)
  o Suggest some options that might resolve the issue (Step Four: Identify Possible Options)
- Over time, their (and your) confidence should increase to the point that they are able to:
  o Put forward their recommended solution (Step Five: Evaluate Options)
  o Consistently select the best and/or most appropriate solution (Step Six: Decide Best Solution)
- When escalating a "true escalation", at a minimum, they need to be able to explain:
  o What the issue is and why it's an issue
  o The cause of the problem and the solution selected. May also want the reasons why it was considered the best solution
  o What has been done already as part of the implementation
  o What is blocking further implementation
  o What help is required to ensure the implementation is successful
- When escalating an "in the loop" issue, a quick summary of:
  o What the issue was, why it was an issue and what was done to resolve it

o   Anything else the manager might need to be aware of, in case it's brought up with them by colleagues, more senior levels of management, clients or other third parties

As part of Specific, we have mapped out a broad sense of what "good" looks like. For any given industry, organisation and function, this can be further enhanced to capture specific needs or nuances, such as timeframes and urgency, quality, regulatory implications, etc.

In summarising a generic objective's Specific, it might look something like this:

SPECIFIC: Resolve vast majority of typical issues that arise within the role by identifying and implementing appropriate solutions, given relevant factors [can be expanded]. When escalating issues, they are signposted appropriately and the relevant information is provided.

By taking the time to reflect on what the specific objective is, you are really setting out your expectations around problem-solving and escalation.

MEASUREMENT

Since this is a behavioural objective, how exactly will success in this objective be measured? Fortunately, as we have a pretty good idea of what success will look like, the steps of problem-solving and the valid categories for escalation, measuring the success of this objective is relatively straightforward.

Chances are you are never going to be able to measure exactly how many issues are actually solved by the individual or how many are escalated. What we do know is that far fewer issues should be escalated, and when they are, they will be appropriately signposted and presented. That shift, in and of itself, will free up a lot of your time.

How can we define Measurement? There are a few different ways successful achievement of this objective can be measured, depending on the person's starting point. Measurement could be framed in some of the following ways:

-   Reduction in number of escalations, e.g. reduce escalations by 50% (useful if there are an excessive number of escalations)

- Number of times issues are escalated as a percentage of the number of issues sorted out (the lower the better)
- Issues resolved appropriately, i.e. don't blow up into a bigger issue down the line
- Number of times appropriate recommendations are offered (the more the better)
- 90% of typical issues resolved; 10% escalated
- Number of times manager is caught out by peers/boss (the lower the better)

If putting a percentage on the number of issues resolved vs. escalated, this could be calculated via a tracking spreadsheet, an issues log or through the emails they send to you (or to whoever is the most appropriate person), which are being used as a mechanism to keep you, as their manager, in the loop.

In addition, when we come to Timeframe, we will see how the themes of "trust" and "confidence" are built into the process. This means that by the time the individual is successfully resolving most issues, we will be confident in and trust they are making the best choices with the information available at the time.

Over time, the tracking becomes less important as the trust, confidence and experience build up. The pattern of behaviour naturally shifts and the new desired pattern becomes the established way of working.

ATTAINABLE

The easy answer here is, "Yes, of course it's attainable. Why wouldn't it be?" but as we acknowledged in Chapter Four, breaking this dynamic might not be 100% within the staff member's control. For a manager that recognises they love nothing more than to sort out a problem, they will need to change their immediate impulses in order to support this objective. If they don't, the objective may not actually be attainable. Another example is a manager who never seems to have time to deal with an issue or to coach the staff member through the issue. If the manager doesn't invest the time to coach the individual, it is also unlikely to be attainable.

So, while strictly speaking, yes, this objective should be attainable, taking time to reflect on the current dynamics may help pinpoint what supports need to be provided. Here are some of the more typical pointers:

- For all managers, they need to ensure that they are holding the line in relation to the individual presenting the escalation in terms of the correct categorisation, i.e. true escalation, help/sounding board, or keeping in the loop. It will take a while for the individual to get into this habit. If they don't signpost the category and you, as their manager, don't pull them up on it (in a nice way, of course. Humour goes a long way here), they are highly unlikely to build the habit.
- For managers that enjoy nothing more than sorting out a problem, they need to find some mechanism or trigger that stops them from jumping in. At a minimum, they need to give the individual permission to point out that the manager is getting too involved, which isn't the role they agreed the manager would play. More importantly, when the individual does point out that the manager is taking over, the manager needs to retreat graciously.
- In this new pattern, the manager is very much the coach. A good coach requires excellent communication skills. They need to ask pertinent questions, actively listen to the responses, listen to and pick up on the non-verbal cues. Since the manager most likely knows the various different aspects that need to be examined and/or taken into account, they need to ask questions that prompt the individual to think of aspects they haven't considered.

Such questions might sound like, "What are the knock-on impacts of that recommendation?" "Have you considered xxxx?" or, "How might other stakeholders react?" The types of questions and the order in which they are asked are very important. The manager needs to commit to using their skills of communication effectively to ensure this objective is attainable. It may become apparent that this is a skill that the manager may need to brush up on or hone. In reality, for this to be attainable the manager will have to commit to supporting the individual through asking powerful coaching questions.

WHAT'S THE IMPORTANCE OF ASKING QUESTIONS?

Before we go on, take a minute to answer this question—why is the ability to ask questions so important? Regardless of what answers you came up with, the core reason of why asking questions is so important during learning is the impact it has on the brain. What did your brain do when you were asked the above question (or indeed, even this question!)? The typical response is that your brain engaged in the thought process necessary to answer the question. Asking a question actively engages the brain with the content, meaning you're more likely to remember the answers.

Now take a minute to clear your mind and then reread the answer given above in the next sentence.

Asking a question makes the brain engage in the thought process and find the information necessary to answer the question.

Now examine the impact reading the answer has on your brain. Most likely, you read it but you didn't engage with the content to anywhere near the extent you did when you had to answer the question. Reading an answer is a passive process while having to answer a question is an active process. While you read it, you could also have been thinking, *What will we have for dinner?* or, *I wonder where the cat is,* or, *Am I nearly finished this chapter?*

Okay, perhaps you're more focused when you're reading a book than when someone is talking to you. However, when we listen to someone talk us through the finer points of project management or marketing strategies, it is very easy for the brain to drift off and start composing the shopping list. The result is that the active engagement with learning that needs to happen, to be able to use the knowledge again in a similar situation, hasn't happened, even though the point has been explained. By asking the person questions that make them think about the finer points of project management or marketing strategies, they are much more likely to assimilate that knowledge and context into their knowledge base and use it again in similar situations. In summary, asking questions—good, giving answers—bad.

Of course, the impact of the above point is that it takes a lot longer to draw the learnings out of a person than it does to just tell them the answers. What about a manager who wants to just "tell" them what to do and not take the longer route of asking questions and prompting the learning? This thinking falls into the realm of the Tortoise and the Hare. The manager that just wants to get the task "done" and isn't thinking of the wider development and enablement of their team aligns with the hare—done and gone; but what happens when there are too many things to be done? Who's available to step in and help?

For the manager who takes a bit longer to get the task done but is also developing their team, as things get busier they now have two or three people on their team able to do the task. This approach is more akin to the tortoise—steady as she goes but better able to deal with more eventualities and ultimately be more successful and effective.

RELEVANT

The overall relevance of this objective is that the individual is able to do all aspects of their job rather than parts of it while other people finish the rest of it off. While some individuals might not see this as that important to them, in time it limits their opportunities. What is the impact of the last ten or twenty percent of their job being finished off by someone else without the individual being aware that this is happening? Firstly, they will think they are doing a good job when, in reality, they're doing an okay job. This is likely to cause friction during performance reviews. The individual doesn't understand why they are getting a middling review. The reviewer is frustrated that they, or someone else within the team, has to pick up 10-20 percent of this team member's role.

Secondly, should they get promoted (and there are lots of reasons as to why a company would promote such a person), they will bring a blind spot into their next role. They may overlook aspects of a process because they were never aware of those aspects in their old role. In the short term, this might be fine, but over time, if those aspects really did need to be done, the lack of knowledge and awareness will come back to haunt the individual, their team, their manager, the business and possibly even the client.

How does that dynamic play out in real life? Let's take a look at what happened to John. John, a maintenance engineer, carried out a monthly service test on a building's pipes system. The process involved running five tests. Depending on the outcome of two of the tests, an additional test might also be required. When John completed the five tests the first time, he shared the results with Sam, his manager. Sam took them from him while muttering something about the possibility of a sixth test being required. When John asked if he needed to do anything, Sam said he would take care of it.

In reality, John should have known how to interpret the results. He should also have known what triggered the need for the sixth test, how to complete it and decipher the results. However, Sam never bothered to explain any of this. He just went ahead and did the additional test.

Over time, this pattern continued, to the point where Sam stopped even mentioning the sixth test and John forgot all about it. Another year passed and Sam was moved to another department. John was promoted to the manager role, unaware that he didn't have sight of the full process and Sam had never documented it. John trained his replacement, Lauren, on the maintenance process and normal business resumed. Lauren started conducting the tests and notified John of the results, which he just accepted. The knowledge had been lost!

As it turned out, the sixth test was to monitor for a build-up of a certain substance. If this substance was allowed to build up too much, it would cause untold damage to the system pipes, i.e. the lack of doing the sixth test in the short term wasn't going to have any major blowback, or minor blowback for that matter. It would be years before the absence of doing this sixth test was discovered.

Another two years passed and the system started to creak. Something happened that caused an independent contractor to be brought in to take a look. Several tests later, it was determined that the build-up of the substance damaged the system irreparably and the whole system needed to be replaced, at a cost of millions.

Recalling how the original pattern emerged, regardless of what Sam's intentions were, it arose because he unilaterally decided to take over doing the last two or three steps of the process. Maybe it was because "it was faster" or because "he really liked doing that task". Regardless of the reason(s) why, Sam never explained to John what those steps were, their importance, or how to do them. This ended up costing the company millions and seriously damaged two people's reputations—John's and Lauren's. You may think this story is far-fetched, but it's based on a true story.

The point here is around relevance and why the need for issues and problems to be resolved at the level they are supposed to be sorted out is so important. John's story is a great example of what happens when individuals are let off doing certain tasks and aspects are done by individuals in other roles. The organisational system goes out of kilter. Done enough times by enough teams across a company and the company's organisational system comes under serious pressure. Over time, the impact gets harder and harder to deal with and can seriously undermine the company's performance.

RECAP ON RELEVANCE

Bringing it back to the individual and SMART, Relevance can be linked directly to their own performance in the role, i.e. the more issues you can resolve yourself the better able you are to do the job. Relevance could also be indirectly linked back to the skills and knowledge required in future roles, as they develop their career. As we have already seen, a core skill of management is the ability to resolve issues. The better the individual is at demonstrating this the more it will help their career aspirations.

In both of these cases, Relevance is framed in general terms of why an individual should engage with developing their problem-solving skills. What about a case where perceptions have already been established about an individual's ability to problem-solve and escalate effectively?

Depending on the individual and which step(s) they are struggling with, they could already have a reputation that they need to acknowledge and reflect on. In this case, Relevance could be framed in terms of how a lack of stepping into sorting out problems is damaging their current reputation and how they are perceived by others. For example, someone who is a good problem-identifier is perceived as only able to find problems and not solve them. This is unlikely to endear them to senior managers and could impact their career. Another example is someone who is good at what they do but is not confident and so appears hesitant, rather than proactive. Again, senior management could have a perception of them as not demonstrating initiative.

Of course, care needs to be taken when discussing relevance in these situations. Different social and organisational cultures approach delivering such feedback in different ways. Some European cultures, such as the Netherlands and France, tend to provide direct feedback straight up, while such an approach would be anathema in Ireland and the USA. If required, using the coaching skill of asking powerful questions can help you to structure the conversation so that they come to the realisation themselves, rather than having to actually utter the words yourself.

TIMEFRAME

As explained in *SMART Objective Setting for Managers* and recapped in Chapter Four, this step is used to map out how the objective is going to be achieved over a series of weeks or months. Designing this step depends on the person's starting point on the eight steps of problem-solving and/or the three valid reasons for escalation. For example, if they're starting from Step two, it could take several months to work through the various steps. If starting from Step five, it will be a lot faster.

Given that there are so many variables, over the next four chapters we are going to coach Trish through the process of designing specific developmental SMART objectives for each of her team members, based on the analysis she carried out in Chapter Five: Diagnosing the Starting Point. These examples will provide more detailed Timeframe plans.

SUMMARY

In summary, we used the SMART model to explore what a generic developmental goal might look like. We considered what elements are actually included in setting such a goal, such as how many issues we actually expect a team member to be able to resolve to successfully achieve the objective. We also explored how we expect different types of valid escalation to be signposted. We then considered some of the different methods that could be used to measure how successfully it was achieved.

We also started considering the causes of the current dynamics and their impact on the attainability, or otherwise, of such an objective. There was a recognition that some aspects might be within the individual's control but other aspects firmly sit in the manager's court.

As the manager, the relevance of why the change in approach needs to happen should also start being reflected on, e.g. what's the business impact? The actual relevance needs to be linked to what is relevant to the individual as this is a behavioural-type objective. Finally, while Timeframe will be used to map out a plan as to how to develop the required skills and confidence, it will depend on each person's starting point.

PROMPTS FOR YOU

Revisit each of the five elements of SMART; identify and consider what aspects are important for you to include, e.g. measuring success, ideal outcomes, etc., within the context of the team, function, organisation and industry.

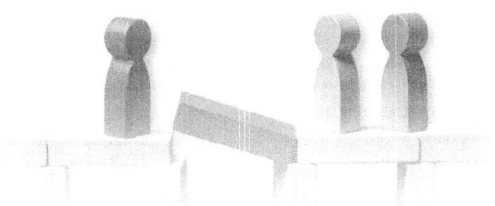

CHAPTER 7

Designing Merv's Ideal Objective

The next four chapters are where the magic will happen. We're going to play coach and ask Trish powerful questions to pull all the pieces together and take a first cut at designing the ideal problem-solving objective for each of her team members. She can then use them as the basis for developing each team member. She can choose whether that's through formally agreeing an objective with each of them and tweaking accordingly or by using the objective outline as a guide to informally coaching them.

As a reminder of Trish's analysis of each person's starting point, here's a recap of Table 5.2: Problem-Solving Team Analysis Summary:

Table 5.2: Problem-Solving Team Analysis Summary Recap

	8 STEPS OF PROBLEM-SOLVING	TEAM MEMBER NAME	COMMENT
1	Identify and recognise problem		
2	Evaluate the size of problem	Merv	Focus on solving problems
3	Research the causes of problem	Damon	Improve issue diagnosis?
4	Identify potential options	Ericka	Bring in creativity?

5	Evaluate potential options		
6	Decide on best solution	Lisa	Build up confidence
7	Implement best solution	Carla	????
8	Review outcomes		

As we can see, Trish's analysis shows that Merv's struggles seem to start at step two. Trish figures that if she can design a suitable objective for Merv, she'll be able to tweak it and design suitable objectives for the rest of the team, so she decides to start with him.

DESIGNING MERV'S SMART OBJECTIVE

Coach: So, Trish, you've decided to start with Merv. What's going on with him?

Trish: Merv is my problem-identifier. Great at identifying an issue. Not so great at deciding if it's a mountain or a molehill.

Coach: Right, so where do we need to get Merv to?

Trish: Over time, I need him to be able to actually sort out a decent chunk of his own problems and only escalate the really big ones to me, but I know he's not going to get there straightaway. In the short term, I'd love if he were able to evaluate the size of issues, be able to decide which ones to look into further and start researching what's causing those ones.

Coach: Okay, if we were to set this out as a SMART objective, the S might look something like:
Specific: To resolve 90% of typical issues that arise within role; to make recommendations as to best solution and reasoning for issues being escalated
How does that sound?

Trish: It sounds great, but he's not going to be able to get to that point straight off!

Coach: You're absolutely right, he won't. It will take him a while to build up to this. But what we're doing here is setting out the end goal. We'll set out the development plan and timeline when we get to Timeframe.

Trish: Oh, okay, that makes sense.

Coach: Good! Moving onto Measurement, how do you want to measure this goal?

Trish: Hmm, could we say something like:
Measurable: 90% of issues resolved, only 10% of issues escalated?

Coach: We could. How would you measure that or at least get some level of measurement?

Trish: Well, for a start, he'd stop coming over to my desk twenty times a day! I'd definitely notice that!

Coach: That would be a good outcome, for sure! That could also be a way of measuring success here—that once Merv is fully up and running, he's only escalating issues to you once a day. Two or three times a week would be even better!

Trish: Oh, that sounds like bliss. What I would do for that…

Coach: Getting back to it, if we agreed to go for tracking how many issues he is resolving vs. escalating, how might you measure that?

Trish: Well, he needs to keep me in the loop, right?

Coach: Yes.

Trish: Well, I could have him email me what the issue is, the size, what he did to resolve it or if he's asking for help. Then I'd get a good sense of which issues he's resolving and how many he's escalating. Would that work?

Coach: Yes, it could well work. Just out of interest, how many emails do you think you might be getting a day from him?

Trish: Oh, right, quite a lot. I'm not sure I want to be inundated with emails either!

Coach:	I didn't think so. Is there a way he could put them all into one file and email you once at the end of the day?
Trish:	Yes, he could. He could compile a sort of RAID spreadsheet. You know that technique that's often used in projects? What's it stand for again? Risks, Assumptions, Issues, Dependencies. Something like that?
Coach:	I think that's what it stands for. Yes, you could agree something similar with Merv. It could be something like Issue, Assumptions, Size, Options and Recommendation. What would that look like—IASOR? Ugh. If we changed it to Problem, what would that give us? PASOR. Yep, PASOR sounds a lot better than IASOR. Let's go with that one.
Trish:	Great. I could get him to pop his problems into a PASOR spreadsheet and email it to me once a day. I could live with one daily email. It would also be a good way to track recurring issues and perhaps try to find longer term solutions to some of those, freeing up the team's time even more. Okay, that's how we'll measure this one. What did we say again?
Coach:	Oh, that's right! Leave me to do all the hard work! (Laughs) I think we agreed something along the lines of: Measurable: Daily PASOR email, summarising issues of the day, roughly 90 percent showing Merv's proposed recommendations while the other 10-ish percent to be escalated.
Trish:	Yeah, that's a good summary.
Coach:	One obvious question. Does this work with your team's workflows, deadlines, etc.? A daily email wouldn't necessarily suit every industry.
Trish:	Good question and the answer is yes, it does work for us. The team's tasks are usually completed over a few days so doing a daily email would work. I suppose if it was an urgent issue, Merv could just come to me straightaway and capture the issue as an escalation, when he's completing his spreadsheet.

| Coach: | The other obvious question is how much time will Merv be using to write up these PASOR issues? |
| Trish: | Well, as it stands, he's already wasting loads of time identifying all these tiny issues and then telling me all about them. So, he's wasting a fair bit of my time already. If nothing else, having a spreadsheet I can glance through would save me heaps of time. That said, I strongly suspect that if he has to go off and research all these little issues, I'd say a lot less of them will be identified. His trick will be to make sure he can tell the difference between all the molehills and the actual one or two mountains that he really does need to identify. |

| Coach: | Excellent. Right, getting back to SMART, is this Attainable? |
| Trish: | Yes, yes, it definitely is attainable. Other people can do it so he should be able to do it too. |

| Coach: | Okay, but will he get the coaching and support he needs to be able to resolve issues on his own? Will you give him the time? Will you be able to break your habit of jumping in and solving the issue for him? |
| Trish: | Yeah, I'm going to have to learn to bite my tongue, but I'm going to need to do that with everyone on the team, aren't I? To be honest, I just can't continue with the dynamic as it currently is. It needs to change and if I need to do something different to allow that change to happen, then I'm just going to have to make sure I change. Did you mention earlier in the book that you had something on that for me? |

| Coach: | That's a fairly definite response. Pain getting too much for you? |
| Trish: | It sure is! |

| Coach: | That's good to hear because, at times, you're going to have to remind yourself of *that* pain and the choices you're making in order to break this habit. And to answer your question, we will be looking at your mindset in Chapter Twelve. We need to finish off designing the team's objectives first. Okay, you have me convinced that this is attainable. So, we have: |

| | Attainable: Yes, with agreed changes and supports. |
| Trish: | Sounds good! |

| Coach: | We're on to Relevance now. How is this relevant for Merv? What's the impact? |
| Trish: | It's relevant to him because it's diverting his attention away from getting things done and it's also slowing other people down too. It's also not good to be constantly focused on what's wrong rather than focusing in on what's right. It drains other people. |

| Coach: | How are we going to capture that? |
| Trish: | Err, could we say something like:
Relevance: Issues taking more resources and time to resolve than they really need to take and preventing other tasks from being done? |

| Coach: | Yes, that would work. You'll probably need to be ready to discuss that further, as you're walking through this with Merv, should he want to. I'd suggest you have some powerful coaching questions ready, to get him thinking. |
| Trish: | Powerful coaching questions? Like what? |

| Coach: | Well, if it was me, I'd have a few questions ready that would prompt Merv to come to a similar conclusion as you, such as: |

- What do you think is the impact of an issue just being escalated up to me without any research being done? Or
- What is the impact of treating all issues equally, without having a sense of which ones are more impactful than others?

Asking a few questions like that would prompt Merv to think about the impact of the pattern of his behaviour beyond his knee-jerk "issue—escalate" that's currently going on.

Again, by asking questions that prompt him to engage in the process of reflecting on what is going on, he is more likely to get and accept the point rather than you just telling him. You telling him gives him the opportunity to "accept or reject" your theory. His coming to these conclusions through carefully guided questions means he is less likely to reject his own conclusions. Just be ready to respond with additional follow-up questions as he puts forward his views.

I'd also suggest having a couple of examples in your back pocket, in case he asks for them.

Trish: Okay, got it. I should just take my time and focus on asking probing questions if he starts questioning the relevance of this and why the pattern needs to change.

Coach: That's it. Right, we're on to the biggie here—Timeframe. How are we going to slice and dice this one? What's the first stage of developing this skill?

Trish: Err, well, first things first. Merv has no problem identifying potential issues, so what he needs to start doing is, for every issue he identifies, he needs to articulate why this is an issue and evaluate how big the potential impact is, right? I also think he needs to go as far as researching what is causing the issue in the first place. I think I'd like him to have that done too before he puts it on the PASOR list.

Coach: Good. That's a great start. Stage one is to have determined the size of the issue and what is causing it. If we link these back to the Eight Steps of Problem-Solving, which steps is stage one capturing?

Trish: Which steps are being covered in stage one? Let me see... Step one is identifying a problem; step two is evaluating the size of the problem. That's included in this stage. Step three is researching the causes of the problem, so we're saying that step is also included in this stage. Now, what's step four? Identifying potential options. No, that step isn't included. So, we're including steps two and three in stage one.

Coach: Excellent, the first three steps are covered. What does stage two look like?

Trish:	For stage two, I want him to start thinking of potential options to solve the issue. At some stage, I would also want him to start recommending what he thinks is the best solution.
Coach:	Great. So which steps are we going to include in stage two?
Trish:	Err, step four definitely. Step five is to evaluate potential options and then step six is to decide on the best solution. I think I might hold over steps five and six to later stages.
Coach:	That might be a wise decision. Before we move on to later stages, what's going to allow Merv to move from stage one to stage two?
Trish:	Sorry?
Coach:	What's going to allow him to move from stage one to stage two? How are you going to interact with him differently so that he is allowed the space to build up his confidence that the points he identifies and considers are the right points?
Trish:	Oh, wow, I hadn't really thought about that. Well, I suppose when he brings me an issue and the size of it, I need to … ask him questions … to get him thinking?
Coach:	Yep, that's it. You need to ask questions. And what's the purpose of those questions?
Trish:	The purpose of the questions?
Coach:	Put another way, how will you know what types of questions to ask? What are you seeking to achieve by asking Merv questions?
Trish:	I'm asking him questions that … that … get him thinking about what things he thought of?
Coach:	Yes, that's one purpose—you want to get a sense of what aspects and elements of the issue he thought of. What else?
Trish:	There's more?
Coach:	C'mon Trish. You know there's more!

Trish: Alright, alright! What other purpose would I have of asking questions? Let me see... Well, I suppose I would also want him to start thinking about aspects that he didn't identify. Would that be another purpose?

Coach: That's it. You want to use the power of questions to get Merv to think about aspects of the issue beyond what he is currently able to identify. What do you think will happen over time?

Trish: Over time, I suppose he would start identifying all the relevant aspects. So he'd end up being able to identify all the aspects that I would normally think about.

Coach: That's exactly right. When Merv gets to that point, what step will he have mastered?

Trish: Well, he will still be in stage one, but he is able to comfortably complete steps one, two and three, identify, evaluate size and research causes.

Coach: And when the two of you get to the stage where Merv has thought of all the right aspects, what else do you think will have happened?

Trish: What else will have happened? Err, let me think. If it got to the point that Merv was able to think about all the different aspects of the issue that I would have identified, what would happen? Well, I'd be thrilled, I'd be genuinely delighted!

Coach: And what else?

Trish: What else? I'd be... I'd be ... comforted that he was thinking of all the right stuff.

Coach: And can you put another name on that?

Trish: I'd ... I'd ... trust that he was thinking about all the right things, just like I would!

Coach: Bingo! You'd trust him. You would trust that what he's coming up with is exactly what you would come up with. And what do you think would be going on for Merv?

Trish: Going on for Merv? What do you mean?

Coach: Well, your trust in him would be increasing, which you'd be naturally demonstrating. So, what would that mean for Merv?

Trish: Well, his confidence in his own analysis would start building, I guess.

Coach: Yes, that's it. He would start building up his own self-confidence that he knows all the various different things he needs to consider to be able to properly resolve the issue. By the way, *HOW* would he know your trust in him is building?

Trish: *How* would he know? How would Merv know that I'm starting to trust his ability to identify the right issues to solve and what to consider when researching them? Hmm, well, when he brings the issue to me and starts to go through the nuts and bolts of it, I would be asking fewer questions, wouldn't I?

Coach: You got it in one. As he brings an issue to you and explains it to you, even if you don't specifically acknowledge it to him, he will pick up that you are asking fewer questions because he has thought of all the relevant things you would think of.

Trish: Right, that makes sense.

Coach: Of course, sometimes it's nice to just openly acknowledge it, rather than making him have to work it out himself.

Trish: Yes, okay, well, now that I know the sequence of events and what I'm looking for, I'll keep that in mind!

Coach: Excellent. Okay, one final question on stage one. When will all this wonderful coaching and learning take place?

Trish: How do you mean "when"?

Coach: Well, if we recap, Merv will complete the PASOR list and email it through to you. Presumably you will need to spend some time with him, going through the items he has put on the list. So, the only question is when will that conversation take place?

Trish: Oh, right, yes, I suppose I will need to go through the items on the list. I suppose I would need to meet with him regularly enough. Possibly daily, to start with. Now, do I want to meet him first thing in the morning or last thing in the evening? If I meet him in the morning, I'll have more energy and I'll be refreshed, but I might be thinking about it all night. If I wait 'til late afternoon, my patience might run out, due to my being tired after a long day. Lunchtime? Oh, just after lunchtime, around 1:30 p.m. would be good. It's usually fairly quiet and I won't be hungry. Okay, 1:30 p.m. every day. I'm assuming it won't go on forever?

Coach: I'm assuming it won't either. However, if it does, Trish, it will likely signify that you are dealing with something more than just not understanding how to progress through the problem-solving steps.

Trish: Okay, let's not even go there yet. I'm definitely all for giving people the benefit of the doubt.

Coach: Good, delighted to hear that. To summarise, you're going to meet with Merv every day, for maybe two to three weeks, and go through the PASOR list he has compiled. As part of preparing the list, he needs to evaluate the size of each potential issue he identifies. We are hoping he comes to the conclusion that perhaps not everything is an issue and that he starts naturally trimming the number of issues down.

He will then need to explain what is potentially causing each issue. As he explains these, you're going to ask him questions, to probe the size of the issues, if necessary, and mainly to ensure that he properly identifies and understands the various different elements that might be causing the issue. Over time, he will absorb these discussions and start explaining to you exactly what is causing the issue and cover out all the elements that you would include yourself.

Great, so at this point, Merv has completed stage one and is now able to size the impact of the issues he's so good at identifying. He's now able to recognise which ones really matter and which he can comfortably ignore. He also has a pretty good sense of what aspects to include when doing his research. Your trust in him is building, along with his self-confidence. For stage two, we said we want him to start coming up with options. You will likely need to signal to Merv that he is moving from stage one to stage two. How will you do that?

Trish: I think I would signal it by making a comment along the lines of, "Well done, Merv, you're doing a great job of understanding what is causing these issues. Now I'd like you to take it a step further and start thinking about the possible options available to sort the issue out."

Coach: Sounds good. Does he still need to complete the PASOR list?

Trish: For the moment, I think so, but I suppose I could play that one by ear. I think it will really depend on how much progress he makes.

Coach: That sounds reasonable. When he does start coming up with options, how are you going to respond?

Trish: The same way I did before. Ask questions to broaden his thinking and understanding.

Coach: Perfect. As this stage progresses, what is also happening?

Trish: His understanding of how to identify the options is expanding, my trust in him is building and his self-confidence is growing.

Coach: Top of the class for you! If I remember correctly, he's now coming to the end of stage two. What steps did that stage cover?

Trish: Stage two just covered step four: Identify Potential Options.

Coach: Did we agree what you want to see in stage three?

Trish: No, I don't think we did. In stage three, I would definitely want to see Merv evaluating options and, at some point, I'd want him to start offering which option he would recommend.

Coach: You're going for top of the class here, Trish!

Trish: If I'm putting in all this effort, I might as well go the whole hog!

Coach: Fair enough. Which steps would be included in this stage?

Trish: Definitely step five: Evaluating Potential Options. Then, when he's comfortable with that, I think I'd like to ask him to start also giving his own recommendation as to what he thinks is the best solution. So, that would bring in step six: Decide on the Best Solution too.

Coach: Do you actually want him making the decision or making a recommendation?

Trish: At some point, I'd like to think that he would make the right call in most cases. These aren't huge, departmental or cross-functional decisions he's making. They're typically smaller issues that need to be recognised, understood and decided, right?

Coach: Well, you'd know better than me but, from what you've said, it would seem that the types of decisions he is likely to make are smaller, in-role decisions. Are some team members in roles that are expected to make those sorts of broader-impacting decisions?

Trish: I suppose a couple of them would be, so maybe that will come up when we address their developmental needs.

Coach: We'll keep an eye out for that and ensure we capture it appropriately. So, where were we with Merv? Ah yes, he was moving from stage two to stage three and evaluating the options. What's the end game here, for Merv?

Trish: The end game is ... for Merv to ... be able to solve most of his own issues.

Coach: Right, so at the end of stage two, he's able to regularly cover out step four and identify suitable options and in stage three he is moving into step five and starting to consider possible solutions. So how are we going to get him to transition into that final step six and be able to decide on the final solution?

Trish:	I know I said this is what I want from stage three, but it's so far away from where he is now I can't even see it! I suppose I need to be thinking about this eventuality though. Well, to get him to start thinking about solutions, I would want him to start … suggesting possible solutions? Or, wait, start recommending to me what *he* thinks is the best solution. How about that?
Coach:	Yep, that's it. At some point, we want Merv to be able to start thinking about what he thinks is the best solution while building up his self-confidence and your trust in his final analysis. So, that would mean…?
Trish:	Back to asking probing questions, to make sure he's thinking of all the potential options, evaluating them all, thinking of the knock-on impacts and being able to sift through it all to come up with a reasonably good recommendation?
Coach:	Good answer, padwan!
Trish:	Thanks. Now, where does all that leave us?
Coach:	Good question! Will we summarise it all into one SMART objective and then see if we're done or if there's anything missing?
Trish:	Excellent idea. Okay, so far, we have the following:

MERV'S PROBLEM-SOLVING DEVELOPMENT OBJECTIVE

SPECIFIC:	To resolve 90% of typical issues that arise within role; for issues being escalated, to make recommendations as to best solution and reasoning
MEASURABLE:	Roughly 90% of issues resolved, only 10% of issues escalated, as initially captured on PASOR
ATTAINABLE:	Yes, assuming we both adjust to our new roles

RELEVANT: Too many issues are being escalated, without sufficient understanding of size or cause of issue. Knock-on impacts on other people's focus and ability to complete their workload

TIMEFRAME:
STAGE ONE: Steps two and three. For issues identified, Merv to evaluate size of issue and research causes and capture in PASOR file. Present to Trish daily, as agreed, and discuss the size and causes of each issue

STAGE TWO: Step four. Identify a range of potential options that might resolve the issue and present for discussion

STAGE THREE: Steps five and six. Start evaluating the options and which ones are more effective than others. In time, present recommended solution

Have I got everything captured?

Coach: In stage three, I'd add in "with reasoning" at the end.

Trish: Right, so it becomes "Along with presenting possible solutions, presenting recommended solution with reasoning"?

Coach: Yes.

Trish: Okay, yeah, I gotcha! I want to make sure that, when he's putting forward his recommendation, I know that he's thought of all the aspects I'd think about!

Coach: That's it. Again, this allows you to understand what he is and isn't taking into consideration as he's evaluating the options and identifying the best solution. If he's missed something, again, the powerful questions kick in. As he absorbs the learning from your interactions, one day, he is going to bring you the issue, why it's an issue, what's causing it, what the options are, what he recommends and why. At that point, you're going to say, "Go in peace, I couldn't have done it better myself." And both of you will walk away from that conversation feeling fantastic.

Trish: I can't see it myself, at the moment, so I'm just going to have to take your word for it.

Coach:	Stick to the approach and trust me; one day, it will happen. Mind you, if it turns out there are other issues such as he isn't assimilating the knowledge or you just jump in and give him the answer, you're right, it won't work. It does take effort on both sides, but it's well worth it when the effort pays off.
Trish:	Hmm.
Coach:	Moving swiftly along, are we done with this?
Trish:	No, we haven't put any timeframes on the plan. How long should each stage last?
Coach:	Great question. This is really going to depend on the complexity of the issues that Merv typically deals with, how regularly they crop up and how long it takes to learn all the aspects to take into account. In some industries and/or roles, each stage could take a couple of weeks. For other industries and/or roles, it could take longer. I have a sneaking suspicion I know what you're going to say for the frequency question, but what about the complexity and how much needs to be considered?
Trish:	Yeah, frequency isn't an issue, so we'll have lots of opportunities to practice this! Complexity, hmm, I'd say about 60% is fairly vanilla and straightforward. It shouldn't take too long to knock those on the head. About 30% is of middling complexity. I'd say that they happen regularly enough that a month or two should be enough time to have seen sufficient examples of them for Merv to be able to resolve most of them. So that leaves us with about 10% of issues in the complex bucket.
Coach:	Well, that makes sense then, with the overall objective. Those complex issues probably equate to the 10% of issues that we're acknowledging will need to genuinely be escalated. The difference here is that Merv will have properly researched them and sought out some options to solve them, rather than just bringing them to you straightaway.
Trish:	Ah yes, we've come full circle. I like it.

Coach: Okay, so maybe we need to add those categories of problems into our objective. We could adjust the Specific to acknowledge them and then we can reference them in Timeframe. So, for each stage, what would be reasonable timeframes to work through them?

Trish: How many stages do we have? Three, and then we need to add in the final pivot before we get to the stage of being confident in Merv's ability. Okay, so four in total. I think he should be able to move through each stage in about four weeks. No, wait, I think with stage one he identifies so many issues that I think he should be able to work through that stage in about two weeks. Then I'd give him four weeks for each of the other stages. How about that?

Coach: Let's get all these changes captured into the objective and then we can take a final look. Right, so we now have:

MERV'S REVISED PROBLEM-SOLVING DEVELOPMENT OBJECTIVE

SPECIFIC: To resolve 90% of typical issues that arise within role; for issues being escalated, to make recommendations as to best solution and reasoning

MEASURABLE: Roughly 90% of issues resolved, only 10% of issues escalated, initially captured on PASOR

ATTAINABLE: Yes, assuming we both adjust to the new approach

RELEVANT: Too many issues are being escalated, without sufficient understanding of size or cause of issue. Knock-on impacts on other people's focus and ability to complete their workload

TIMEFRAME:
STAGE ONE: Steps two and three. For issues identified, Merv to evaluate size of issue and research causes and capture in PASOR file. Present

to Trish daily, as agreed, and discuss the size and causes of each issue [weeks 1–2]

STAGE TWO: Step four. Identify a range of potential options that might resolve the issue and present for discussion [weeks 3–6]

STAGE THREE: Steps five and six. Start evaluating the options and which ones are more likely than others. In time, present recommended solution, with reasoning [weeks 7–10]

STAGE FOUR: Consistently resolve 90% of issues within his role

Coach: Is that it? Is that the full objective?
Trish: Yep, I think so.

Coach: Are you sure?
Trish: From that question, there's clearly something missing!

Coach: Well, what do we want after stage three? Looking at this, in weeks 7–10, we're expecting Merv to be able to put forward his recommended solution. Once he gets to the point where he is consistently putting forward the right recommendations, as far as you're concerned, do you still want him coming to you with the issue and recommendation?
Trish: Eh, well, I suppose I don't. Is that the right answer?

Coach: It is, but *why* is it the right answer?
Trish: Well, because at that stage I'll trust that he'll make the right decision and select the best solution.

Coach: And?
Trish: And I won't want him to be wasting his or my time telling me all that…

Coach: But?
Trish: But … I … still … need to know what's going on?

Coach: That's it. What you don't want to start happening is that Merv becomes overly confident and starts making decisions that you're finding out about six weeks later, when something blows up!

Trish:	No, I *definitely* do NOT want *that* to start happening! The irony of that! So, I would need him to keep me in the loop?
Coach:	Exactly. Stage four is that, from week 11 onwards, or whenever you both agree he's ready for that stage, he should be ensuring that he's keeping you in the loop. You could use that PASOR idea, if you wanted. What you might also find is that the trust and confidence, on both sides, has built up so much that that's not even needed any more.
Trish:	Oh, I'm soooo looking forward to *that* day!
Coach:	So, do we need to revise the objective specific?
Trish:	Whaaaaat! Why do we need to do *that*?
Coach:	Well, I'm looking at it and we never put anything in about sign-posting the purpose of an escalation. We didn't capture that point when we were doing Specific at the beginning. Also, are we happy to assume that the issues that Merv does resolve are appropriate responses and not just quick, "get something, any-thing, done" type solutions?
Trish:	Why are you only mentioning this now?
Coach:	It's an iterative process, Trish. It's highly unlikely you'd get everything captured first time. And that's perfectly okay. Mind you, the more you do it the quicker you get, I swear!
Trish:	Humph! I'll take your word for it. Right, so let's go with some-thing like the following:

MERV'S FINAL PROBLEM-SOLVING DEVELOPMENT OBJECTIVE

SPECIFIC:	Resolves 90% of typical issues that arise within role; for issues being escalated, appropriately signposts the reasons for the esca-lation. For a sounding-board/help escalation, explains issue and makes suitable recommendations as to best solution and pro-vides reasoning to back up recommendation

MEASURABLE: Roughly 90% of issues resolved appropriately, only 10% of issues escalated, as initially captured on PASOR

ATTAINABLE: Yes, assuming we both adjust to the new approach

RELEVANT: Too many issues are being escalated, without sufficient understanding of size or cause of issue. Knock-on impacts on other people's focus and ability to complete their workload

TIMEFRAME:

STAGE ONE: Steps two and three. For issues identified, Merv to evaluate size of issue and research causes and capture in PASOR file. Present to Trish daily, as agreed, and discuss the size and causes of each issue [weeks 1–2]

STAGE TWO: Step four. Identify a range of potential options that might resolve the issue and present for discussion [weeks 3–6]

STAGE THREE: Steps five and six. Start evaluating the options and which ones are more likely than others. In time, present recommended solution, with reasoning [weeks 7–10]

STAGE FOUR: Consistently resolves 90% of typical issues, while keeping manager in the loop on a timely basis. For escalated issues, appropriately signposts the reason for the escalation, makes appropriate recommendations, based on full understanding and explanation of the issue, and shares reasoning behind recommendation [from week 11 onwards or as agreed]

Trish:	Happy?
Coach:	Delirious! You?
Trish:	Happy. I think I can commit to this. I do have one more question though.
Coach:	Okay, shoot!
Trish:	Do I actually share this objective with him?
Coach:	That's a brilliant question and it really depends on how you want to introduce this new approach. We'll work through this in a lot more detail in Chapter Thirteen. In the meantime, what

	we are doing here is using the SMART framework as a way of diagnosing where each team member might be starting from and how we might approach developing them, from where we think they are starting in the problem-solving process. It's very hard to coach someone, whether in sport or in business, when we don't know what either the starting point or the end-goal look like. In the case of problem-solving, it's even harder when we don't have a clear picture of the steps we need to bring them through to get from A to B!
Trish:	That's *so* true! I had never stopped to think of all the different steps I go through when I'm solving a problem. It's just so automatic! So, just to summarise what you said, at the moment, we're using SMART as a way to get a good handle on where each person is starting from and later I'll decide how I best use that information?
Coach:	I'd just make one slight adjustment to that summary. We're getting a good handle on where we *think* each person *might* be starting from. Depending on how you approach the introduction of the new approach, you might need to ask some questions to check if your starting point assumptions are correct.
Trish:	Oh yeah, that's a good point!
Coach:	One final point to mention. You've just worked through designing a SMART objective for Merv who, we suspect, is getting stuck at step two: Evaluating the Size of the Problem. Right?
Trish:	Right!
Coach:	Having done all this work, we should work through each of the other team members a lot faster, as they'll be starting somewhere closer to the end goal.
Trish:	Oh, great point! I think somewhere in the back of my mind was a niggle about having to do this amount of work for all the other members of the team too. But I can see how I've done a lot of the heavy lifting with Merv.

| Coach: | Great. I think we're happy with Merv's objective so let's move on to the next person on your list. |
| Trish: | Happy to! |

SUMMARY

On the basis that the earliest starting point is working with an individual that is able to identify when a potential issue has arisen, i.e. step two, we applied the SMART framework to Merv's developmental need. We recognised that while we needed to develop his ability to work through each of the first six steps of problem-solving it needs to be broken down into manageable stages.

The Timeframe of the SMART framework allowed us to set out the different stages and which problem-solving steps were included in each stage. In relation to the attainability of this objective, we recognised that it is attainable but it may require changes in approach from both Merv and Trish. Trish needs to be as committed to changing this dynamic as Merv. In this case, Relevance for Merv is more to do with the impact of his behaviour on Trish. Most likely, he is completely unaware of its impact on Trish. As we consider Relevance for other team members, it is likely to change substantially.

By asking questions, we coached Trish through the process while ensuring she was designing an objective appropriate to her company, function, team and industry. As you read through this chapter, there may be times when Trish's response might not have been totally appropriate for your situation. That's okay and to be expected. This isn't a formulaic approach of "do A, then B followed by C and you'll always get D". Rather, it is to understand what the purpose is and explore appropriate ways we might get there.

If you work in a faster, more immediate environment, the PASOR idea might not work. So, you might need to identify an alternative way to capture and deal with the issues. Remember, you can always leverage the team's ideas as part of the process of introducing the new approach. Start as you mean to go on!

Trish now has a very clear picture of what a SMART objective, to develop Merv's developmental needs, might look like. She hasn't yet decided whether she is going to share this with Merv, as a formal objective, or whether she is going to use this knowledge to informally coach him through the stages.

PROMPTS FOR YOU

Given the cadences and levels of complexity in different industries and functions, it is highly likely that some of Trish's responses wouldn't work for your own situation. Re-read the chapter and identify questions where you felt Trish's response wouldn't be applicable in your workplace.

Using the Prompts for You worksheet, note down those questions and:

- Write down your own answers
- Consider how your answers might impact the various elements of the final SMART objective that would work in your situation/industry
- Make appropriate adjustments to the objective, so that it is tailored to your particular needs

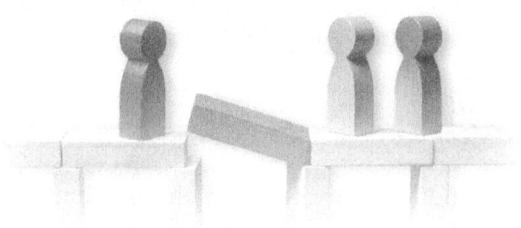

C H A P T E R   8

Exploring Damon's and Ericka's Development Needs

Following on from Chapter Seven, Trish is now going to use the objective she designed for Merv as the basis for designing appropriate objectives for each of the other team members. She pulls out her team analysis summary again, to see who's next up, and it's Damon.

Table 5.2: Problem-Solving Team Analysis Summary Recap

	8 STEPS OF PROBLEM-SOLVING	TEAM MEMBER NAME	COMMENT
1	Identify and recognise problem		
2	Evaluate the size of problem	Merv	Focus on solving problems
3	Research the causes of problem	Damon	Improve issue diagnosis?
4	Identify potential options	Ericka	Bring in creativity?
5	Evaluate potential options		
6	Decide on best solution	Lisa	Build up confidence

| 7 | Implement best solution | Carla | ???? |
| 8 | Review outcomes | | |

As coach, let's explore with Trish what Damon's developmental needs are and how they can be addressed.

DAMON'S OBJECTIVE NEEDS

Coach: So, Trish, what's going on with Damon?

Trish: Okay, what I have noticed with Damon is that he seems to offer what he thinks is the right solution, but when I look into it further, it turns out he hasn't really understood what the issue is. He might have gotten half the issue or suggested a related solution that doesn't address the actual issue. That's why I put him at step three, because he doesn't seem to properly research or understand the cause of the problem or diagnose the real issue. Unlike Merv, there is usually a valid issue, so I guess he senses that the issue is sufficiently big enough to be addressed. He just doesn't quite figure out what the right issue is. Does that make sense?

Coach: I think so. Would I be right in saying that he knows that there's an issue but, rather than figure out exactly what the issue is, he goes straight to solution mode?

Trish: Yeah, that sounds about right. Perhaps if he better understood what the issue was, he might actually be able to identify the right, or at least a better, solution. Having gone through a few of these situations with him, I suppose at this stage, I don't even give him the benefit of the doubt.

Coach: Yes, several rounds of that pattern playing out and I can see how your response could easily become a habit. If we take a look at Merv's objective, what point do you think Damon might be starting from?

Trish: Right, I have Merv's final objective here. Let's take a look:

MERV'S FINAL PROBLEM-SOLVING DEVELOPMENT OBJECTIVE

SPECIFIC: Resolves 90% of typical issues that arise within role; for issues being escalated, appropriately signposts the reasons for the escalation. For a sounding-board/help escalation, explains issue and makes suitable recommendations as to best solution and provides reasoning to back up recommendation.

MEASURABLE: Roughly 90% of issues resolved appropriately, only 10% of issues escalated, as initially captured on PASOR

ATTAINABLE: Yes, assuming we both adjust to the new approach

RELEVANT: Too many issues are being escalated, without sufficient understanding of size or cause of issue. Knock-on impacts on other people's focus and ability to complete their workload

TIMEFRAME:

STAGE ONE: Steps two and three. For issues identified, Merv to evaluate size of issue and research causes and capture in PASOR file. Present to Trish daily, as agreed, and discuss the size and causes of each issue [weeks 1–2]

STAGE TWO: Step four. Identify a range of potential options that might resolve the issue and present for discussion [weeks 3–6]

STAGE THREE: Steps five and six. Start evaluating the options and which ones are more likely than others. In time, present recommended solution, with reasoning [weeks 7–10]

STAGE FOUR: Consistently resolves 90% of typical issues, while keeping manager in the loop on a timely basis. For escalated issues, appropriately signposts the reason for the escalation, makes appropriate recommendations, based on full understanding and explanation of the issue, and shares reasoning behind recommendation [from week 11 onwards or as agreed]

Trish: Okay, so taking a look, the Specific stays the same. That's probably going to stay the same for all of them, isn't it?

Coach: Yes, it's very likely to, with a couple of exceptions. I'm not sure what will emerge with Carla and Jaime. I suspect their issues are a little bit different.

Trish: Intriguing! We'll focus on the rest of the team first and then we'll take a look at Carla and Jaime. So, Measurable … yes, that pretty much stays the same. I'd be only delighted if Damon sorted out 90% of the issues that crop up in his role. Attainable, yep that's still good for Damon. Okay, next up, Relevant… Right, this one is going to have to change a bit, isn't it?

Coach: Yes, the Relevance for Merv doesn't work for Damon. So, what's the business impact of Damon's pattern of behaviour?

Trish: Hmm, what is it that Damon does and what is the business impact of it? He definitely identifies issues that really are genuine issues, but then he offers up a solution that doesn't actually solve the issue. Why does that matter? Em, well, if he actually implemented his suggested solution, he'd be wasting a lot of time and resources and then still end up with the original issue. In fact, he would probably have made things worse because he would have lost time and now he would most likely have two issues to sort out.

Coach: So, to paraphrase, you're saying that he's wasting time and effort to end up two steps behind instead of one step forward?

Trish: Yeah, that's a good way to paraphrase it. Ending up two steps behind puts him under pressure and then he's not able to finish work or meet deadlines.

Coach: I'll play devil's advocate here and pretend to be Damon. In response to this, I'd say, "Why can't you sort out the problem at that point?"

Trish: Well, I can't keep sorting things out because it's unnecessarily distracting me away from other work I need to do. If I get involved in all of these issues, we might eventually end up one step ahead, but I'd be three steps behind. No, no, no, that's just not going to work. It would be a lot better if he took more time to research and understand the issue and find the right solution instead. It might slow him down, but at least he'd end up one step ahead. I'd be happy if he even ended up at half a step ahead because at the moment, when everything is taken into account, we're probably ending up three or four steps behind.

Coach: Right, do you want to summarise the Relevance for Damon?

Trish: I'll do my best. The Relevance for Damon is that he needs to take the time to properly research and understand the real issue and then identify the right solution to the right issue, thereby being more effective with his time. Something like that?

Coach: Not bad. I thought you were going to mention backward-and-forward steps there.

Trish: (Laughs) No, I was beginning to think I was in a game of Snakes and Ladders for a minute!

Coach: Okay, for our immediate purpose, it will do for the moment. You might decide to finesse it a bit more or it might naturally develop a bit further, based on your chat with Damon, when you're discussing this with him. Last, but not least, we have Timeframe. What, out of this, do we need to keep?

Trish: Hmm, this is an interesting one. With Merv, he needed to evaluate the size of the issue and then research the causes. With Damon, he also still needs to research the causes and then move on to suggesting possible options to solve them. Now, do I want him to practice those steps separately or all in one stage?

Coach: That's an excellent question, Trish. What are the pros and cons of keeping them separate or combining them?

Trish: Straightaway, a definite pro to combining them is that it should reduce down the time it will take for him to work through the stages. A con is that he might not build up his confidence in his ability to research the right issue. Or more likely, *I* might not build up *my* confidence in his ability! Actually, now that I've said that out loud, I definitely want to keep them as separate steps. What do you think?

Coach:	I think that, if you're having that strong a reaction to the impacts of putting the two steps together, it's a very good idea to keep them separate. That way, you'll know if there is a more fundamental issue going on in his ability to research and grasp the essence of the real issue and its causes. Just to say, with someone else it might be fine to combine the two steps. What would the next stage be?
Trish:	I think the rest of it pretty much stays the same. Oh, that's interesting; the only aspect that really changed for Damon was the Relevance!
Coach:	Yes, that and that he doesn't need to identify the size of an issue. Do you want to summarise Damon's final objective, there?
Trish:	Sure; Damon's final objective looks like this:

DAMON'S FINAL PROBLEM-SOLVING DEVELOPMENT OBJECTIVE

SPECIFIC:	Resolves 90% of typical issues that arise within role; for issues being escalated, appropriately signposts the reasons for the escalation. For a sounding-board/help escalation, explains issue and makes suitable recommendations as to best solution and provides reasoning to back up recommendation
MEASURABLE:	Roughly 90% of issues resolved appropriately, only 10% of issues escalated, as initially captured on PASOR
ATTAINABLE:	Yes, assuming we both adjust to the new approach
RELEVANT:	Rushing into solving "a" problem, rather than "the" problem is causing knock-on effects and slowing work down. Taking time to properly research and understand the real issue and then identify the right solution to the right issue will result in more effective use of time

Timeframe:

Stage One: Step three: For identified issues, research root causes and present to Trish, as part of explaining the issue [weeks 1–2]

Stage Two: Steps four & five: Along with presenting root causes, start presenting options for possible solutions [weeks 3–6]

Stage Three: Step six: Along with presenting possible solutions, present recommended solution [weeks 7–10]

Stage Four: Consistently resolves 90% of typical issues while keeping manager in the loop on a timely basis. For escalated issues, appropriately signposts the escalation, makes appropriate recommendations, based on full understanding and explanation of the issue, and shares reasoning behind recommendation [from week 11 onwards or as agreed]

Trish: You were right!

Coach: About what?

Trish: About two things. One, that Relevance needed to be finessed. I'm happier with what I've written here. Also, I'm happy to include the idea of "root cause". You were also right about how much faster designing Damon's development plan went, having done all the heavy lifting with Merv's objective.

Coach: Ah, yes, it did go a lot faster, didn't it? Great, I think we're done with Damon, are we?

Trish: Yes, I'm pretty happy with that. Similar but with subtle differences to Merv's.

Coach: That's it. Who's next up? Ericka? What's her story again?

Trish: Okay, so the story with Ericka is that she's good at identifying potential issues, she researches them well and has good understanding of what's causing them. She does come to me with suggestions, but what I find is that her suggestions are fairly basic and they're not the most imaginative. We have a value of Innovation and I really couldn't say that her recommendations are exactly cutting edge. Oh, the other thing is that I've found myself in a few meetings lately where it has turned out that

Ericka has gone ahead with a solution and not said anything to me about it. Not the worst complaint, I guess, but since we're doing this…

Coach: Sure, in for a penny, in for a pound. If you're going to put in all this effort, you might as well go for gold here and develop Ericka's abilities in all aspects. And no, not the worst, but what you have done is identify that she still has room for development. It sounds like we've a couple of issues going on here. What do you think they might be?

Trish: Well, issue one is Ericka needs to increase her creativity in coming up with a good solution. So, not so much step four and identifying possible options, although there might be a little bit of that going on, but I think it's more in her ability to evaluate possible solutions and perhaps mash them together into a broader solution. Maybe the issue lies in a combination of steps five and six. As I think about what I see her doing, it's like she takes the obvious answer, rather than examining all the different perspectives and aspects, putting them all into the pot and seeing what emerges. Does that make sense?

Coach: It definitely sounds like she could push herself more in her thinking, and if she did, it is likely she would come up with better solutions.

Trish: Yes, I sense she can do better. It might turn out I'm completely wrong, but I really do think there's more there. Right, you mentioned there were likely a couple of issues going on with Ericka, so let me take a minute and see what the other issue might be. Err … I think the other issue is around the reasons for escalation. She's not keeping me in the loop. If I remember correctly, there was no particular issue about the solutions she did implement. Nothing came back to bite. Probably not the most imaginative, but we've already captured that point. It was more to do with me being left in a situation where I wasn't aware of what had happened.

Coach: Yes, this was the other area I was thinking of, so well done for identifying it. Now the question becomes: what's the business impact of both the lack of imaginative solutions and the fact that she's not consistently keeping you in the loop?

Trish: What's the business impact? Err, well, in relation to the creativity, the solutions Ericka is likely to come up with will probably be fine but won't take a broader view or take potential opportunities to really improve the process. So, I guess, we get short-term, sticking-plaster-type solutions rather than gaining advantage from the possibly better outcomes that we might get with a more creative solution. What's the business impact of that? Well, we don't really improve things; we just trundle along, similar to what we were doing.

Coach: It sounds like the business impact here is the lost opportunity costs. The issue has to be resolved anyway, but with a little bit more effort, Ericka could come up with a better solution and the team would benefit; the client, other teams, etc. could potentially benefit as well.

Trish: Yeah, that's a good summary of what I'm getting at. So, in relation to her not keeping me in the loop, I suppose the business impact is that it doesn't look like we're working as a team. Why does *that* matter? Well, it matters because if other teams start to give people in our team work and they sense that we're not necessarily talking to each other, two people on the team could end up doing the same piece of work and we would end up with duplication. Or it could cause issues if I, or someone else on our team, has said, "No, we're not doing that," and they then go and ask someone else in the team to do it, knowing there's a good chance we won't have talked to each other... Now that I think of it, it has the potential to be quite impacting to the team.

Coach: Excellent. I don't know if that would or wouldn't happen, but I'm delighted to hear there's a bigger impact than you just wanting to know everything going on because you like to feel in control. Well done. The fact that you could explain it in terms of a valid business impact means that the concern is well enough founded to matter. Let's take a look at what Ericka's objective would look like, shall we?

Trish:	Yes, great, it feels like we're making real progress in understanding where each of the team members is coming from. I'll do like I did before and copy over Damon's and use that as the basis for adjusting Ericka's. Does that make sense?
Coach:	Sounds like a good plan.
Trish:	So, Damon's final objective was as follows:

DAMON'S FINAL PROBLEM-SOLVING DEVELOPMENT OBJECTIVE

SPECIFIC: Resolves 90% of typical issues that arise within role; for issues being escalated, appropriately signposts the reasons for the escalation. For a sounding-board/help escalation, explains issue and makes suitable recommendations as to best solution and provides reasoning to back up recommendation

MEASURABLE: Roughly 90% of issues resolved appropriately, only 10% of issues escalated, as initially captured on PASOR

ATTAINABLE: Yes, assuming we both adjust to the new approach

RELEVANT: Rushing into solving "a" problem, rather than "the" problem is causing knock-on effects and slowing work down. Taking time to properly research and understand the real issue and then identify the right solution to the right issue will result in more effective use of time.

TIMEFRAME:

STAGE ONE: Step three: For identified issues, research root causes and present to Trish as part of explaining the issue [weeks 1–2]

STAGE TWO: Steps four & five: Along with presenting root causes, start presenting options for possible solutions [weeks 3–6]

STAGE THREE: Step six: Along with presenting possible solutions, present recommended solution [weeks 7–10]

STAGE FOUR: Consistently resolves 90% of typical issues while keeping manager in the loop on a timely basis. For escalated issues, appropri-

ately signposts the escalation, makes appropriate recommendations, based on full understanding and explanation of the issue,
and shares reasoning behind recommendation [from week 11
onwards or as agreed]

Trish: So, am I good with the Specific? I'm not sure. It doesn't say any-
           thing about keeping me in the loop on issues that she's happy to
           sort out. Do I need to include that somewhere here?

Coach: Have you taken a look at the Measurable?

Trish: Measurable… It says that most issues should be sorted and cap-
           tured on PASOR. What was PASOR again?

Coach: It was that spreadsheet that we were going to get Merv to fill
           in and email to you. It stood for Problem, Assumptions, Size,
           Options and Recommendations. If I remember correctly, we
           were also going to use it as a communication tool, to keep you
           in the loop, as he got better at sorting out issues.

Trish: Ah yes, of course, Merv is the "problem-identifier man" and
           excellent at it. That was one way of getting him to recognise
           the sheer number of issues he identifies on a regular basis. Do I
           really want to use that tool for Ericka? I'm not sure I do. To be
           fair to her, she sorts out a lot of issues well and there's no real
           need for her to even come to me with them.

Coach: Out of curiosity, what's the difference between the majority of
           issues Ericka sorts out and doesn't tell you about and the ones
           that have happened recently that have resulted in you question-
           ing her lack of keeping you in the loop?

Trish: That's an excellent question! What is sufficiently different
           between those two scenarios? Well, in the scenario that doesn't
           bother me, Ericka is working on tasks that are within the team's
           remit. They are to do with how we organise our work and deliver
           it. So, I have no major issue with her sorting out stuff within her
           role or within the team. The problem, now that I think about
           it, is when she sorts out issues that go cross-functional. That's
           when I start to get nervous. I don't get the sense that she thinks

84

about all the different perspectives and the knock-on impacts. Yet she is potentially agreeing to something that the team is going to end up bound by. Okay, that's it, that's when I get really concerned and that links back to my concern about the quality of the solution and the lack of innovation or creativity. Yeah, that's it!

Coach: Well, that certainly throws a new light on your concerns about Ericka. So, if I may paraphrase this back to you, Ericka needs to broaden her perspective and understanding from focusing only on her own role or what the team does to focusing on understanding the team's role within the wider organisation and she needs to consider solutions from a broader organisational perspective, rather than just whether your team can or can't do something?

Trish: Yes, that's it. You know yourself, sometimes other teams or functions are just trying it on, to see if they can chuck something over to our team. If something makes sense that it sits within our team, that's absolutely fine. I've no problem with that. However, there are times when us taking on responsibility for a particular task makes no sense. It actually sits better with the other team but they don't want to take it on. It's *those* sorts of situations where I want to ensure that the proposed solution makes sense.

Coach: If I can summarise that point, rather than just agreeing to other teams' requests, Ericka needs to consider whether she is committing the team to taking on tasks that might not actually fall into the team's areas of responsibility. Does that capture it?

Trish: Yes, that's it.

Coach: Phew, I thought we were nearly finished with Ericka and then all *that* came out!

Trish: As I'm working through this, I'm realising how subtle all this is. If you hadn't asked me that question, I'd have never realised that it was those situations that I was concerned about. And look, I've definitely proved it wasn't just my need to feel in control!

Coach:	I'll *definitely* grant you that one! So, where *does* that leave us with Ericka's objective? Does it make any sense to use PASOR with her?
Trish:	No, I don't think it makes sense to use it with Ericka. I think I want her to be sorting out issues within her role, as she has been doing, and if she feels she needs to tell me or escalate something to me, because she needs a sounding board, that's all good.
	I think that, when it comes to issues that cut across teams or functions, or solutions that will have knock-on impacts on our team and/or other teams, at a minimum she needs to keep me in the loop, but for the moment, I actually want her to bring them to me, to explore them. I want to understand her thinking and prompt her to start thinking more broadly. So, I know I need to use a similar approach to what we discussed with Damon. It's just the content will be somewhat broader. Does that make sense?
Coach:	Perfectly. And what about the quality of the solutions? The innovation? How do you want to deal with that?
Trish:	Oh, yes, good thinking. How do I help her develop that? Would I send her on a course? For creativity? Design thinking, maybe? Or when we're exploring the options, could I ask her questions to point her in some alternative directions? I'm open to ideas here!
Coach:	They are all potential options and something for you to have a think about. You could also consider using the plus-two tool. So, when Ericka has shared her thoughts on the available options, you could ask her to come up with another two options; that would likely push her beyond the obvious of what she can see.
Trish:	Oh yeah, that could help. Would I include that tool in her objective?
Coach:	If you're going to use the objective as a guide for you, to coach her through the process and develop her broader problem-solving abilities, I'd suggest not. If it was me, I'd just introduce it

at an appropriate time and start using it. Since you mentioned that the organisation has a value of Innovation, I'd couch it in terms of wanting to increase the team's innovation in solutions. That could go for the whole team, since the value applies to everyone.

If I was setting it as a formal objective, as part of Ericka's performance management objectives, I'd probably include a point about recommended solutions incorporating some level of innovation or creativity. I would then connect the Relevance for the need for innovative solutions to the organisational value of Innovation. Does that make sense?

Trish: Yes, so I have a few different options, depending on whether I introduce it formally or informally and how I think supporting Ericka through the development process might work best.

Coach: That's it. There are guidelines but, again, this isn't the type of process that "if I do A, followed by B and C, it will automatically result in D". There are too many variables in how effectively A, B and C are done. Some of it is in the skill of identifying where the issue might be arising from while some of it is in the skill of introducing and framing the developmental need and moving the individual through the process. Some of it is the skill of inviting the individual into the conversation and co-creating an approach so they feel part of it and not having the solution "done to them"! Never a good thing.

Having clarified all that, shall we take another cut at Ericka's objective?

Trish: Yes, back to square one … or is it square two? Eh, no, it's definitely square one. Starting with Specific, I'm going to adjust this as follows:

SPECIFIC: Resolves 90% of typical issues that arise within role or cross-team/functional; for escalated issues, signpost appropriately.

For a sounding-board/help escalation, explains issue, identifies possible options while incorporating some innovative ideas, makes suitable recommendations as to best solution and provides reasoning to back up recommendation.

MEASURABLE: Roughly 90% of issues resolved on own, approx. 10% of issues escalated. For cross-functional/team issues, solutions should have no major impact on team, unless approved by manager.

Coach: Very good. If that's the Specific, where are you going to address the developmental aspect of this?
Trish: In the Timeframe, of course!

Coach: Just checking!
Trish: Nice try. I know Specific and Measurable are used to describe the end outcome! Okay, so is it attainable? Yes, I'm happy with what's there. As for Relevant, we've definitely got this one nailed. Let me capture both of those now.

ATTAINABLE: Yes, assuming we both adjust to the new approach.

RELEVANT: Need to prevent agreeing to cross-team/functional solutions that inappropriately bring work onto our team when the solution doesn't really make sense in terms of the broader organisational picture. Need to actively demonstrate the value of Innovation in solutions.

Trish: Just Timeframe left now. What do I want here? For issues within her role that she's happy to sort out, for the most part, I think I'm happy that she just resolves them. If there's a major concern, she can bring it to me and I've got that covered out in the 10% escalation of issues. So far, so good. In relation to cross-team/functional issues, I definitely want her to have understood it, researched it, identified and considered options. Do I want her to be bringing recommendations? Err, I don't think I do, initially. In time, I definitely do, but initially I think I just want her to go as far as step four: identifying possible options. That way,

I'll be able to ask questions to get her thinking more broadly. If I ask her to bring recommendations and they're not ideal, I'll only be knocking her recommendations back. Okay, I have it! I want to see the following:

TIMEFRAME:

STAGE ONE: Steps three & four: For cross-team/functional issues, research and understand issue and present to Trish, along with two to three possible options plus two [weeks 1–4]

STAGE TWO: Step five: As above, plus suggest two to three viable solutions; include plus two if the proposed solutions haven't started incorporating the creativity [weeks 5–8]

STAGE THREE: Step six: Start to present preferred recommendation, with reasoning [weeks 9–12]

STAGE FOUR: Consistently resolves 90% of typical issues, either within her role or cross-team, while keeping manager in the loop on a timely basis. For escalated issues, appropriately signposts the escalation, makes appropriate recommendations, based on full understanding and explanation of the issue, and shares reasoning behind recommendation [from week 13 onwards or as agreed]

Trish:	Did I include everything?
Coach:	I think so. I like the way you've assumed the creativity will start to be demonstrated by weeks five to eight but still allow flexibility, in case it hasn't. I'm now curious about why you extended the number of weeks within each stage.
Trish:	Oh, look at you, Little Miss Curious! I have a very good reason that I'll let you in on. I extended it because these issues don't come up as regularly, but I think over roughly a month, we'd have worked through enough to allow Ericka to progress along the stages.
Coach:	Ah, that makes sense. So, dare I suggest we've finished with Ericka's objective?
Trish:	I do believe we have. I'll just capture it all in one place, as follows:

ERICKA'S FINAL PROBLEM–SOLVING DEVELOPMENT OBJECTIVE

SPECIFIC: Resolves 90% of typical issues that arise within role or cross-team/functional; for escalated issues, signpost appropriately. For a sounding-board/help escalation, explains issue, identifies possible options while incorporating some innovative ideas, makes suitable recommendations as to best solution and provides reasoning to back up recommendation

MEASURABLE: Roughly 90% of issues resolved on own, approx. 10% of issues escalated. For cross-functional/team issues, solutions should have no major impact on team, unless approved by manager

ATTAINABLE: Yes, assuming we both adjust to the new approach

RELEVANT: Need to prevent agreeing to cross-team/functional solutions that inappropriately bring work onto our team when the solution doesn't really make sense in terms of the broader organisational picture. Need to actively demonstrate the value of Innovation in solutions.

TIMEFRAME:

STAGE ONE: Steps three & four: For cross-team/functional issues, research and understand issue and present to Trish, along with two to three possible options plus two [weeks 1–4]

STAGE TWO: Step five: As above, plus suggest two to three viable solutions; include plus two, if the proposed solutions haven't started incorporating the creativity [weeks 5–8]

STAGE THREE: Step six: Start to present preferred recommendation, with reasoning [weeks 9–12]

STAGE FOUR: Consistently resolves 90% of typical issues, either within her role or cross-team, while keeping manager in the loop on a timely basis. For escalated issues, appropriately signposts the escalation, makes appropriate recommendations, based on full understanding and explanation of the issue, and shares reasoning behind recommendation [from week 13 onwards or as agreed]

Coach:	Great. To recap, we've done Merv, Damon and Ericka; that leaves us with Jaime and Lisa for this section and then we'll explore what might be going on with Carla. So, it probably makes sense to go with Lisa next?
Trish:	Will we take a break and resume this in the next chapter?
Coach:	Sounds like an excellent plan. See you then!

SUMMARY

By designing the initial objective starting from step two, it makes it a lot easier to design an objective for individual team members, regardless of which step they are likely starting from. However, it is worthwhile taking time out to identify what is different from one situation to another, rather than setting a blanket objective based on which step an individual is starting from. For example, with Ericka, by reflecting on the different types of problems Ericka solves and which ones make Trish nervous, additional insights into the actual concern were highlighted, ensuring that the objective captured the right points while recognising what Ericka did well.

PROMPTS FOR YOU

Going back to the team analysis you completed, as part of Chapter Five, identify team members you suspect are starting at either Step three: Research the Causes or Step four: Identify Potential Options. For each of them, take some time to reflect on what might really be going with them and where they may be having difficulties. Consider what development objectives you would outline for each of them.

Along Came Lisa and Jaime

Coach:	Did we decide if we'd start with Jaime or Lisa?
Trish:	I think you suggested Lisa and I agree with you. Let's start with her. Right, so my concern with Lisa is that she is really, really good at what she does but she doesn't seem to believe in herself. She understands the issue, researches it, considers all aspects, and usually puts forward at least one very viable solution but just doesn't seem to want to take the responsibility for making the decision. If I'm completely honest, I have absolutely no idea as to how I would go about building her up so that she would trust herself. This is about *her* self-confidence because I have every faith in her.

Coach:	Ah yes, the perennial doubter! Okay, so what do you think is really going on here?
Trish:	Oh no, is this one all *my* fault?

Coach:	I have no idea, but if I was a betting person, I'd put money on it not being *all* your fault, if that makes you feel any better.
Trish:	A bit! So, let me think about this. What do I think is *really* going on here? To start at the beginning, I don't know if this only started when I began to manage the team or if it was going

on before that. I know I did say to her that if she needed any help, she should feel free to come to me.

Coach: What was the previous manager like? Do you know?

Trish: Err, from what I heard, he was alright, as a manager. My sense was that he thought he knew everything and I think, at times, he could ridicule people's contributions a little bit. I don't know him so I can't really say too much, but that's just the sense I've picked up.

Coach: Let's assume there's a bit of truth in that. What kind of impact do you think that sort of behaviour would bring out in someone like Lisa?

Trish: Oh, good question. I hadn't thought of that. Eh, I would imagine it would knock her confidence a bit. She'd be quite hesitant of saying too much in case it was ridiculed. She most likely wouldn't want to be the person who made the decision in case it was wrong! I can't imagine that would be fun.

Coach: Good, there's some interesting insights right there. Now, not that lack of confidence or belief is always due to a previous or, for that matter, current manager's behaviour towards them, but it certainly is worth considering and reflecting on.

Trish: I can't imagine a manager that was behaving in that way would acknowledge their own impact on the situation. Would you?

Coach: I can't imagine such a manager would be reading this book, so we don't really need to worry too much about them!

Trish: Touché!

Coach: Where were we? Oh yes, thinking about what might be causing Lisa's lack of self-confidence. So, while we can't always hypothesise where a person's lack of confidence might be coming from, we can help Lisa build her confidence up, or back up, if it's been knocked. Using our approach, any ideas how we might go about this?

Trish: I think we need to focus straight in at step five or six. For the most part, the Specific, Measurable, and Attainable will be the same as Ericka's. The Relevance will change, for sure. As for the Timeframe, I think I could start with asking her to explain the issue right up to step five and her suggesting two to three possible solutions. I'd then ask her questions to explore her thinking. Since I'm quite sure I'd agree with most of her thinking, since I usually do, I would be letting her know that I'm agreeing with her, so that would all be very positive.

Then I think I could start transitioning towards having her put forward the solution she would recommend and her reasons why. I'm assuming that, fairly quickly, I'd end up just more or less agreeing with her the whole time. Then I could tell her that, as part of the explanation and solutions, I want her to start putting forward her recommendation and reasoning. Fairly quickly, she should see that I'm constantly agreeing with her. That must surely build up her confidence, right?

Coach: I think what you're suggesting there is an excellent start to approaching this. I'd imagine that, for most people, assuming the execution of it is done reasonably well, their confidence would start building up, along with your confidence in them.

Trish: What do you mean by "for most people"?

Coach: Well, it could be that for one or two people, there are deeper-seated issues at play that might need to be examined.

Trish: Like what?

Coach: Eh, they could have deep-rooted beliefs (not of the limiting self-belief sort) that prevent them from accessing their confidence. They might have a worldview that means they can't see that they could be as good as someone else at doing something. That said, my starting point would definitely be as you just outlined there.

Trish: And what did you mean by "executing it reasonably well"?

Coach: Well, care would need to be taken to ensure the conversation was mainly positive and that learnings were achieved via a coaching style, asking questions and showing curiosity, rather than by telling. Just telling Lisa that she's well able to sort the issue out isn't going to build up her confidence. She might see that as a brush-off. To succeed in this, you're likely going to need to invest a bit of time in these conversations and not make them feel rushed. However, I'd be quietly confident that you'd make great strides fairly quickly.

Trish: Okay, that makes sense. What if we weren't making progress after a few weeks?

Coach: Do you think that might happen?

Trish: Well, I don't know, but, if it did happen, I'd like to have a sense of what I might need to do at that point.

Coach: If it did happen, I would suggest that very gently, and very much from a position of curiosity, you make an observation statement such as, "I've noticed you don't seem to be too comfortable in putting forward a recommendation or making the final call. What's going on there for you?" and then keep quiet. Keep quiet, even if she says nothing for five minutes and you're only dying to jump in. Just say nothing!

            If you have to do this, make sure you can give it whatever amount of time it requires to properly finish out the full conversation. For example, if you're about to run into another meeting, I'd suggest it's *not* the right time to share your observation.

            Once you had the conversation, you'd have a much better idea of what is really going on for Lisa, which would allow you to respond accordingly. Does that make sense?

Trish: Yes, I can see why you wouldn't go straight for that option.

Coach: No, I'd definitely recommend your option first and, as I said before, that is very likely to work with most people who struggle in this area.

Trish:	Okay, that just leaves us to work through Relevance. Let me just talk out loud for a minute about what I think the Relevance might be for Lisa and then I'll bring it all together into a final proposed objective. At some point, we're going to explore how I'd go about introducing all this to the team and setting out these objectives with them, aren't we?
Coach:	Yes, we will. All will be revealed in Chapter Thirteen!
Trish:	I can't wait! Will I be in that chapter?
Coach:	If you're good! Now get to work!
Trish:	Grumble, grumble, grumble… (Laughs) Okay, so why is this important to Lisa? Well, if she doesn't build up her self-confidence, this is definitely going to be career-limiting. She's going to end up staying in a fairly junior role. There's absolutely no way she'd get much of a promotion if this continues!
Coach:	Oh, and why's *that*, then?
Trish:	Well, because you need to be able to problem-solve and sort things out to be promoted.
Coach:	Ah yes, we've just managed to come full circle on the Manager's Dilemma—the need to be good at problem-solving to get promoted, followed by the dilemma of whether to focus the energy on continuing doing what you were rewarded for or invest time in learning an unproven approach that will empower the whole team's problem-solving!
Trish:	Hmm…. Right, I'm happy with the Relevance point for Lisa.
Coach:	Just before you go into summarising the objective, what if Lisa says, "That's fine, I don't want to get promoted?"
Trish:	Eh, do people *say* that sort of stuff?
Coach:	One or two people have been known to, yes!
Trish:	If she says that then I suppose I'd have to explore with her why not and what the long-term consequences of that might be?

Coach: Good initial response. It might be worthwhile you reflecting on the Relevance point and identifying what other potential impacts there might be that could also help this to resonate with Lisa.

Trish: I will but, in the meantime, I'm going to move swiftly on to summarising this objective:

LISA'S FINAL PROBLEM-SOLVING DEVELOPMENT OBJECTIVE

SPECIFIC: Confidently resolves 90% of typical issues that arise within role or cross-team/functional and keep manager in the loop appropriately; for escalated issues, signpost appropriately. For a sounding-board/help escalation, explains issue and makes suitable recommendations as to best solution and provides reasoning to back up recommendation.

MEASURABLE: Roughly 90% of issues resolved on own, approx. 10% of issues escalated. For cross-functional/team issues, solutions should have no major impact on team, unless approved by manager

ATTAINABLE: Yes, assuming we both adjust to the new approach

RELEVANT: Confidently making recommendations builds credibility and reputation, resulting in developmental and/or promotional opportunities arising

TIMEFRAME:
STAGE ONE: Steps two to four: Along with explaining the issue, start suggesting two to three viable solutions [weeks 1–4]
STAGE TWO: Steps five & six: Start to present preferred recommendation, with reasoning [weeks 5–8]
STAGE THREE: Consistently resolves 90% of typical issues, either within her role or cross-team, while keeping manager in the loop on a timely basis. For escalated issues, appropriately signposts the escalation, makes appropriate recommendations, based on

full understanding and explanation of the issue, and shares reasoning behind recommendation [from week 9 onwards or as agreed]

Trish: How does that sound?

Coach: Yep, sounds good. I see you added in the word "confidently" under Specific.

Trish: Yes, I guess I need Lisa to understand that hesitantly putting forward suggestions or recommendations isn't quite enough. She needs to give the impression she's reasonably sure about the recommendation she's putting forward. I think with my asking questions, showing curiosity and agreeing with her points, her confidence will start to build.

Coach: Excellent.

Trish: What are your thoughts about how I phrased the Relevant section?

Coach: I think that you know Lisa much better than I do, so you'd have a much better idea of the types of words that would speak to her. Keep in mind, as well, that you won't be sitting down with her and just getting straight into reading a pre-written objective. Most likely, you'll have already had a chat about the importance of building up one's ability to problem-solve, touched on the problem-solving steps and then started probing into where she sees her own problem-solving abilities.

Trish: Is this Chapter Thirteen again?

Coach: Yes, now that you mention it, it is!

Trish: Oh, so I'm getting a sneak preview now!

Coach: Only a smidgeon! Who's left, Jaime?

Trish: Nice pivot there! Ah, yes, Jaime, my problem child! Okay, so Jaime just wants to know what to do; I tell him, he's gone and he does it. My issues are (1) he can interrupt me several times a day; and (2) I've noticed that he regularly brings the same issues

	to me, even though I've told him how to deal with the situation before. That's Jaime!
Coach:	Ah, yes. Jaime was the one we couldn't quite figure out where to put him. Right, what do *you* think is going on here?
Trish:	Err, given all I know now, I think he is coming up to me with a narrow problem. As it is a direct question, firstly, I'm just answering it, i.e. I'm giving him the answer. Secondly, because I'm giving him the answer, there is absolutely no need for him to engage with the answer, think about what it means or what the impact of the answer might be. It's that passive vs. active brain-thing in technicolour!
Coach:	Yes, this is a great example of the passive vs. active brain response. Knowing that, what tools do you have available to change this dynamic?
Trish:	Well, one tool is definitely to stop just giving him the answers. Is that a tool?
Coach:	Tool, strategy … I don't get too hung up on the words. It's definitely an approach you can use, which should change the dynamic. What other tools do you have?
Trish:	My questioning tool. Assuming I can bite my tongue and not just give him the answer straightaway, I can start asking questions and get him to think about what exactly he's asking me and spend more time exploring the context.
Coach:	Very good.
Trish:	Okay, so if I started doing that, how would that play out? Jaime comes to me and asks a question. Instead of giving him the answer, I ask him a who, what, why, when type question. He answers and then I have a better sense of what is going on. Then what would happen? I'd likely ask another question, which he would have to answer. This would go on for a bit and, if I do it right, I'll have asked him a series of questions that brings him towards the right answer. That sounds good. Then what would

	I want to have happen? Hmm … I would likely want him to summarise what he is going to do, wouldn't I?
Coach:	That's a good idea. At this point, you're inviting him to use the tool of Summarising, while you get to quality control his comprehensive summary.
Trish:	Yes, so he summarises the discussion, and if he has forgotten a key point or he muddles it up, I'm able to immediately help him work through it again by asking more questions.
Coach:	Excellent. I think that approach should definitely change the dynamic. As Jaime realises that you're not going to just give him the answer, what do you think might happen?
Trish:	I know what I *want* to happen, whether it happens naturally or not! I *want* Jaime to stop coming to me with every little thing; and I know what you're going to say. You're going to say that he keeps coming to me because I keep making it easy for him. Well, I'm definitely all on for changing the rules now and he is going to have to work a lot harder to get the answer. I might even see an immediate reduction in the number of times he comes over to me!
Coach:	That might *well* be a welcome outcome of this. Do you think you'll need to say anything to Jaime about how often he is coming to you?
Trish:	That's a good question. Do I trust that having to work harder for the answer will translate into him coming over to me less? Hmm … decisions, decisions. I could say nothing and hope that it will translate and, if it doesn't, say something then. Or I could say something up front and make it crystal clear. If I was to say something, how might I approach it?
Coach:	Talk me through how exactly this typically plays out.
Trish:	Okay, I'm usually working away on something and Jaime comes over and asks me a question. I answer it. He goes off and does what I've instructed him to do. I am now a little distracted from whatever task I was doing, so I end up checking emails, chatting

to someone, grabbing a coffee. I finally get back into the task and, twenty minutes later, he's back at my desk with another question. The same sequence of events plays out. One or two more times of this and either I have a meeting to go to or I just give up on that task and do something else.

Coach: What's the business impact of that?

Trish: Will I have a rant now or later?

Coach: If I have a choice here, I'll pick later for the rant!

Trish: Ah, you're no fun! In that case, I'll try to keep my answer on an even keel! The business impact is that my task is taking longer to do than it should, if it ever gets done at all! And later, when I should be doing other tasks, I'm not getting to them because I still have this initial task to finish off. My own work builds up and puts me under pressure and that starts putting other people under pressure if they need it quickly. If I leave the task, they start to get irritated with me because I'm not getting something done for them or I haven't gotten back to them with an update. How did I do? Did I stay calm?

Coach: Not bad. I could feel the emotion rise a little, but you kept it pretty steady! Great job on expressing why this dynamic just doesn't work for you or the business. Going back to your question about whether to say anything to him about the number of times he's coming to you, what needs to change here?

Trish: He needs to stop coming over to me! Isn't *that* obvious?

Coach: (Laughs) It is obvious, from your perspective, but what about from his perspective?

Trish: Sorry?

Coach: Well, what if he really does need help? Do his issues have to be resolved immediately or can many of them wait until later?

Trish: Usually, they can wait. The odd one might have some level of urgency about it, but, even then, it could wait a few hours.

Coach: How long has Jaime been in his role and/or in the company?

Trish: Err, let's see, I think he joined about four or five months ago. Why are you asking about when he started?

Coach: I'm asking about it because Jaime is throwing out a lot questions/problems to you, taking the answers and actioning them but not necessarily assimilating the learning and using it again. If he's only been in the role a few months, there is the possibility here that he hasn't been properly trained and he doesn't know enough to anchor the answers you're giving him.

Trish: I'm not sure I'm really following you.

Coach: Well, if you have a body of knowledge and a colleague gives you some additional piece of knowledge, what do you typically do with that new piece?

Trish: Oh, I ... I guess I examine that piece of information in relation to what I already know and adjust my understanding accordingly. I might ask questions, if I don't understand how it relates to, or if I feel it is creating tension with, other things I know.

Coach: Right, I do something similar. Now, can I ask you to think of a topic that you don't know much about but you know a few people who are very knowledgeable about the topic?

Trish: Got one, my dad and his friends are huge into fishing and can talk for hours about it. I know nothing, even though I suppose I should.

Coach: Okay, now, if you asked your dad a question and he gave you the answer, and let's say it's a reasonably technical answer, what would you do with that new piece of knowledge?

Trish: If it was reasonably technical, I don't know what I'd do with it. I possibly wouldn't really know what he's talking about and might not ask him to explain because I'd be afraid he's already told me it before.

Coach: Do you think you'd retain the piece of knowledge?

Trish: Ah, possibly not! But why wouldn't I when I would very likely retain the information in the first scenario? It's clearly not because I can't, so it must be because I don't have the same context for it as I did when I already knew quite a bit about the topic.

Coach: Right, in the first scenario, you could anchor the piece of knowledge in what you already knew, but in the second situation you didn't have the same ability to anchor it. So now you either need to ask a whole lot of questions to properly anchor the knowledge or accept the answer given, even if you don't fully understand it, and hope you remember it just in case you need it again.

Trish: Which, let's face it, is highly unlikely. It's much more likely I'll forget it until the next time.

Coach: Exactly. So, if we bring this back to Jaime, do we think his training has properly equipped him to be able to remember and anchor what you're telling him?

Trish: I'd like to be able to say, "Possibly not", but if I'm being truthful, it's probably a much more definite, "No, it probably hasn't". I was supposed to do a chunk of training with him, but other stuff came up and I never got around to it. Okay, that makes sense. So, what do I need to do with Jaime?

Coach: I think Jaime is going to need some attention, but, on saying that, he can't keep interrupting you. Hopefully, with all the good work you're doing with the others, you'll start gaining back some time, which should leave you with a bit more time for Jaime. So, recognising that (1) you need to give him some more time; (2) he doesn't know enough about his job to be able to sort things out himself and so has lots of questions; (3) you can't continually be interrupted the whole time; and (4) the work Jaime does isn't so urgent and therefore waiting a few hours or until the following day is possible, how might you approach this differently and meet both your and Jaime's needs?

Trish: How about I ask him to note down his questions and we agree a thirty-minute slot every day to go through his questions? A bit like I set out for Merv. but in Jaime's case, the focus is on explaining concepts, sharing knowledge, and training him on the tasks. That way, I can go through his questions but, rather than just answering them, like I am now, I can ask him some questions to probe his understanding and explain the context of what it is he is trying to do. That way, he understands the answers within the context of what he is doing and, hopefully, he should remember it a bit better.

Coach: That's a good suggestion. Of course, in true coaching fashion, I'm not going to just leave it there. What's another way you could approach this?

Trish: (Groans) Another way? Really? I thought I was doing well with that one!

Coach: You did do well with that one, but here's a question for you. In coming up with that answer, where was your attention?

Trish: Where was my attention? Okay, okay, I'll go back to that last question and answer that one! It seems waaaayyy easier than this one! Where was my attention? What do you even mean by that question?

Coach: Where was your attention? Who were you thinking of when coming up with that suggestion? Don't get me wrong. It is a valid and plausible solution. I just want to explore with you where your attention was when coming up with it. What assumptions did you make as part of coming to that potential solution?

Trish: What assumptions did I make? Where was my attention? I suppose my attention was on... Well, now that I think about it, I assumed that I had to be part of the solution. So, my attention was on how I was going to support Jaime, but it doesn't actually *have* to be me, does it? It could be Lisa, or one of the other, more experienced, members of the team. One of them could buddy up with Jaime to explain the task, the context, and answer his quick questions.

Coach: That's it! You are the manager, but it doesn't mean everything has to come through you. I know this is about empowering the team's problem-solving, but it's also about empowering the team to help team members within the team, rather than always having to go the hierarchical route.

Trish: Okay, where does that leave me with Jaime? Is it a problem-solving thing with him or is it a training thing?

Coach: What do you think is driving this pattern of behaviour?

Trish: Now that we've worked through this, I think it *is* coming from a lack of training and if we get that sorted out, the frequency of questions and the number of repeat questions will naturally drop.

Coach: Yeah, that's my sense too. If you focused on this while also introducing the new way of escalating problems and issues, how do you think this might play out with Jaime?

Trish: I think if we can get his understanding of what he's doing up to the right level and, as a team, we've already started the new approach to escalation and solving problems, I think he would naturally absorb that new approach and adjust to it. I suppose we'd need to signpost the gradual shift between being in "training" and "knowing enough to be able to sort out issues yourself" modes.

Coach: I think that's an excellent idea. If you lay out the path as going from "training" to being able to "do it yourself" (more or less) to "experienced and able to sort out most problems" and signal how the expectations change, then Jaime is more likely to naturally evolve along each of those stages. The stages have been explicitly called out for him, so he doesn't need to waste time trying to figure it out himself. This hits upon a really, really important point. Going back to the point about most managers being good at problem-solving, they tend to have a natural tendency to figure things out, which gets them noticed, which results in them being promoted, right?

Trish: Right.

Coach: What would you say came first, the tendency to sort stuff out or that if they sorted stuff out, they'd get rewarded and promoted?

Trish: I'd say the tendency to sort stuff out came first.

Coach: Me too. For the people who don't demonstrate that natural ten-
             dency, does it mean they're not good at problem-solving?

Trish: Oh! There's a good question! Does it mean they're not good at
             problem-solving or does it mean they're not good at taking the
             initiative to solve it without being told? That's really the ques-
             tion you're asking, isn't it?

Coach: Yes, that's exactly the question I'm asking. Does "not nat-
             urally taking the initiative" equate to "not being good at
             problem-solving"?

Trish: My gut response would say, "No, they're not the same thing".
             Someone could be very good at problem-solving and really
             grow into that skill and start taking the initiative, if coached
             and mentored in the right way.

Coach: What does *that* potentially mean for companies?

Trish: Well, it would mean that if we recognised the dynamic that
             happens in front-line management, as we've already explored,
             and if we could break that dynamic, it would mean more people
             would be better able to do their current jobs and, in turn, more
             likely to be considered for promotion. The company would
             have widened its talent pool, meaning they wouldn't have to go
             external as much; they'd retain people longer, naturally reducing
             the cost of people turnover, and everyone would win. It would
             also mean that tasks are completed at the right levels, and the
             actual cost vs. expected cost of tasks would be broadly in line.

Coach: That's it in a nutshell!

Trish: Okay, I was most definitely *not* expecting us to cover all of that
             with Jaime! Where does that leave us with his development?

Coach: Good question. Is the specific for Jaime the same as it is with
             the others?

Trish: Well, no, it's not really, is it? Jaime needs to get up to speed with
             his role and the various tasks in his role, rather than focusing on

his problem-solving skills. At some point, he may need a problem-solving type of developmental objective, albeit we've discussed how he might naturally absorb the process as it becomes embedded within the team. For now, though, his focus is on building up his experience and understanding of the role. How do I do that?

Coach: That's exactly it. What we've done here is recognise that, while we originally included Jaime in the assessment of each team member's ability to sort out problems, he actually shouldn't have been included because he's not experienced enough in his role to be able to sort issues out. More importantly, we've recognised that that's appropriate for Jaime. We could have a situation where a person has been in their role for two years but, due to poor training and lack of feedback, their actual experience and understanding of delivering the role is more akin to how someone with three months' experience in the role might perform. That's a harder conversation because they really shouldn't have been left to languish like that.

Trish: Listening to that, I'm glad I'm getting my head around this now and not in another twelve or twenty-four months.

Coach: Yes, the longer a person is left languishing like that the harder it becomes to resolve. Getting back to Jaime, what might his developmental objective look like?

Trish: I guess it's going to be more focused on him learning his role. How about something like this?

JAIME'S DEVELOPMENTAL OBJECTIVE

SPECIFIC: Confidently master the core tasks of role and consistently deliver them within the required timeframes and to the right standards

MEASURABLE: Deadlines consistently met and rework kept to a minimum

ATTAINABLE: Yes, provided sufficient training is provided

| RELEVANT: | Ability to deliver core elements of role allows time to master broader role and become involved in additional projects, which deepens experience and leads to career opportunities |

TIMEFRAME:

STAGE ONE: Set out core tasks, and assign a team buddy to provide and support training and learning. Agree training plan and expectations [week 1]

STAGE TWO: Implement training plan with a three-way weekly check-in [as per agreed training plan timings]

Coach: That looks really good. I like the way you're not setting an exact deadline now, as to when you expect this to happen, but it will be captured in the training plan, which the three of you will be regularly monitoring. Excellent.

Trish: Phew! Working through Jaime's situation really brings home to me the importance of stepping back and reflecting on what is really going on with the person and not just lumping everyone into the same bucket. I genuinely don't think I would have come to this conclusion about Jaime left to my own devices.

Coach: The most important thing is to be open to taking the time to reflect. Once you know how, it becomes a lot easier and faster. So now we're just left with figuring out what might be going on with Carla. Shall we adjourn to the next chapter?

Trish: Sounds like a plan!

SUMMARY

Some people aren't as naturally confident as others; past experiences might have left them wary or they just aren't as sure of themselves, even though they are competent in their job. They might need a manager who will build them up and help them feel confident that what they do and how they approach things is valid.

Alternatively, if someone doesn't know how to do the basics of their role or understand the context and purpose of their role, they will struggle to anchor additional information into their knowledge base. When training someone into new tasks and/or a new role, it is important to explain the context and expectations so that they can start anchoring the information.

As a manager, in order to fully enable and empower the team, it's important to really reflect on where each member of the team is and what might be going on for them. It's important to take time to look at the world from their perspective and where they might actually be starting from. When in doubt, ask.

PROMPTS FOR YOU

Review your original analysis, completed as part of the Prompts for You Chapter Five: Diagnosis the Starting Point section. Reflect on your team and consider whether any of them might be in a similar situation to either Lisa or Jaime. If you identify someone that perhaps is in a similar situation to either of them, answer the following questions:

- What might this person's perspective be?
- Where might they need to start from?
- What does that mean for you in terms of developing them?

The Curious Case of Carla

Coach:	So, Carla! I've been looking forward to exploring this dynamic since the very beginning!
Trish:	Really? I just don't know *what* to make of Carla! She's very good at what she does. She's able to sort most issues out herself. When she does bring something to me, it typically is an issue that generally does need to be teased out with someone else, but, but, but, this is what has me pulling my hair out... When we've agreed a solution, she may or may not implement it the way we agreed. Much more worryingly than *that*, if she *does* decide to do something different, she doesn't bother letting me know that she's changed it. So, I merrily assume it's done, as per what we agreed, while she's gone off and done something different.
Coach:	I'm assuming you found out the hard way that she's making these unilateral changes?
Trish:	Yes, the *very* hard way! With one of them, it took me days to sort out the knock-on impacts and I was fit to kill. You really wouldn't have wanted to be around me *that* day, let me tell you!
Coach:	I can only imagine! Before I share my thoughts, let me ask you a couple of questions. When you found out that you agreed one

Trish:	solution and Carla implemented another solution, did you ask her why she changed her approach? Yes.
Coach:	Can you remember what she said?
Trish:	Yes, if I remember correctly, on that massive change I just mentioned, she said she was going to implement the solution we discussed but, on her way back to her desk, she started talking to Brad in Accounts. They started talking about the issue and Brad recommended doing something different, so that's what she did.
Coach:	Do you think that in some of the other situations something similar might have happened? That she talked to someone between leaving you and implementing the solution?
Trish:	Err, yes, I remember another time she said she had changed the solution because she had talked to someone else. I can't remember who, but I do recall thinking it was odd that she was ranking their view as higher than mine. That had always struck me as a little strange.
Coach:	Excellent, just as I suspected. If it makes you feel any better, here's what I think is going on with Carla.
Trish:	Please, I'm all ears. Shedding *any* ray of light on what might be going on with her would be helpful!
Coach:	I don't think Carla's issue is with problem-solving. From the sounds of it, she's reasonably competent in her job, knows how to sort most things out and, when she isn't sure, she's escalating them appropriately, to get input from you. What I *do* think Carla struggles with falls into the area of Emotional Intelligence. In emotional intelligence, or EI, there's a concept called "Independence". Independence deals with our ability to remain independent of other people's thinking, ideas, actions and, more subtly, emotions. Someone with high-functioning Independence is able to think independently of other people's thoughts and ideas. They are able to decide how they are going to act, independent of what others are doing. They also don't

get involved in person A's emotional concerns about person B, nor do they let person A's emotions cloud their own views of person B.

On the other hand, someone with low-functioning independence finds it difficult to shape their own thoughts, they are easily led by others and influenced to act in ways that fall in line with how others want them to act. They find it difficult to stand up and say, "No". They'll take their ideas from others and may also be swayed by other people's opinions.

Trish: Okay, and how does Independence relate to what we see Carla do?

Coach: Good question. It can be difficult to relate theory to the behaviours we see on the ground. From what you've said, Carla talks through an issue with you and agrees to implement it. On the way back to her desk, she meets someone else and talks through the issue with them. They suggest she solves it in some different way, perhaps driven by their perspective on the issue, be it personal or functional. If she has low independence, as I suspect, Carla takes what they say lock, stock and barrel and implements that solution. Her low-functioning independence means she doesn't question their motives or perspectives. Nor does she seem to consider how she's going to explain the different approach she took to the one she agreed with you when this inevitably comes to light. Perhaps she's not thinking that far down the road, which, again, would be in keeping with someone with low-functioning independence.

Trish: It sounds like she does whatever the person she spoke to last tells her to do.

Coach: That's not a bad way of thinking about how low-functioning independence can show up in someone when it comes to ideas and actions. Low-functioning independence in relation to emotions tends to show up a little differently.

Trish: If this is what is going on with Carla, how on earth do I even think about an objective to develop her in relation to something like this? Is it even possible to develop or increase a person's independence?

Coach: Great question and, yes, it is possible to develop and enhance one's independence. That's the beauty of emotional intelligence. That's the good news. The bad news is I don't think you're going to be the one who will be able to help her increase it. I think your role is to firstly highlight to Carla that this behaviour is an issue; secondly, to suggest that it might be due to the need to increase her independence and that she might need to work with a coach to help her achieve that; and finally, to get budget approval for her to be able to work with a coach, assuming she agrees to it.

Trish: You don't think I could do this myself, even if you guided me?

Coach: For some aspects of emotional intelligence, I could definitely see that option being a possibility. For example, if we were talking about the need to increase optimism or emotional self-aware-ness. However, with independence, there could be several dif-ferent underlying issues that are feeding into and undermining her ability to remain independent. It could be as simple as not realising that she is being unduly swayed by others. On the other hand, issues such as low-functioning self-regard, another area of emotional intelligence, or a personal value such as Perfection or some unhelpful belief could be the root of the issue.

Given those possibilities, it would be best if a coach experienced in these areas worked with Carla to help her uncover what is really going on for her. If you go this route, I recommend you to be very careful in selecting the right coach for her. Not every coach would be experienced and skilled in this area.

Trish: I think you're right. It sounds like there could be a lot more to developing a person's independence than meets the eye. Can I still design an objective for this?

Coach: On the subject of "eyes", you sure are keeping your eye on the ball with this one! I think you could definitely design an objective something along the lines of this:

CARLA'S DEVELOPMENTAL OBJECTIVE

SPECIFIC: Increase level of Independence, to be able to recognise and consider own thoughts, views, actions and emotions on a topic or person, rather than taking on other people's thoughts, ideas, actions and emotions as if own

MEASURABLE: Able to put forward own views and ideas and explain and stand over reasons for them. If changing them, able to explain why the change should be made, independent of other people's input. Decisions are implemented, as agreed, and not unilaterally changed

ATTAINABLE: Yes, provided Carla is agreeable to coaching and the coaching budget is signed off

RELEVANT: Changing solutions and decisions, based on other people's needs, is damaging Carla's credibility and having knock-on impacts on the business and the team's work

TIMEFRAME:
END MONTH ONE: Agree and sign off on a suitable coach
END MONTH TWO: Source experienced coach and agree coaching programme
MONTH THREE ONWARDS: Commence coaching programme with monthly check-ins

Coach: Of course, this is a back-pocket type of objective. Having a sense of the objective looking something like this, you could use it to guide your conversation with Carla. However, the final objective would emerge during the course of the two-way discussion. While I know Carla likely has low-functioning independence,

	you don't want to be taking advantage of that and railroading her into an objective that she fundamentally doesn't agree to.
Trish:	No, that wouldn't be right either.
Coach:	This is the first objective where the attainability of it depends on something outside of individual team members, including you, having to make a concerted effort to change. It's going to depend on the organisation agreeing to support this, either through a suitably experienced internal coach or investing in Carla by paying for an external coach. Do you think the company will agree?
Trish:	Yes, I don't see why not. We have a budget for training, so I'll just get my manager to sign off on it. We don't have internal coaches in our company but, even if we did, I can't imagine them being experienced enough in dealing with something like this!
Coach:	Perhaps not. You are definitely looking for a coach qualified in emotional intelligence, but you would also want to check out how they approach working with a person to develop and enhance their EI. Well, congratulations. Four chapters later, I think we've finally worked through the nuances of each member of your team, except one!
Trish:	One? Who's that?
Coach:	You, of course! We've examined the various different scenarios of what could be going on for each of the individual team members. We can't leave you out! However, before we go and explore the manager's problem-solving mindset, I thought we would make one final stop and explore some bonus outcomes that can potentially be tapped into after all this hard work. Is that okay with you?
Trish:	Absolutely, let's go. Anything to push out examining me and my mindset!

SUMMARY

Sometimes, there are issues beyond understanding the steps of problem-solving, correctly applying the tools of different steps of problem-solving or being confident in executing each of the problem-solving steps. Aspects such as emotional intelligence, beliefs and values can also play into one's ability to effectively sort out problems.

As we saw with Carla, having a low-functioning ability in a specific area of emotional intelligence resulted in her being unable to stick to her guns and do what was agreed. In these situations, designing an objective that highlights the need to change the behaviour and stating the business impact as to why the change is necessary should be done. However, it is likely that the skills and expertise needed to deal with these sorts of issues are beyond the experience of most managers. Providing the expert support required for the individual to achieve objectives in this space is something that is best left to executive coaches experienced in these areas.

PROMPTS FOR YOU

Consider if there is a "Carla" on your team. It is someone who can typically work through the different steps of problem-solving and/or apply the various tools of problem-solving but you still have a concern about how they approach implementing solutions.

If you do have a potential "Carla", note down the observable behaviours and the business impact of those behaviours. In Chapter Twelve: The Manager's Problem-Solving Mindset, we will cover out some additional models that can impact on how we show up, such as Assumptions, Beliefs, etc. Once you've read that chapter, review your notes from this Prompts for You exercise and reflect on whether any of them might be potentially relevant to this person's situation.

Consider if you think you can discuss this with your team member or if you would need external support. If you need external help, reflect on what it might look like and how best to obtain it.

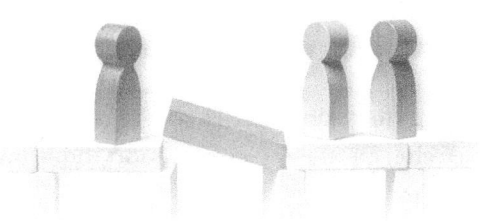

C H A P T E R   1 1

Bonus Outcomes

Trish:	So, do tell all on the bonus outcomes!
Coach:	Okay, I have two bonus outcomes from all this hard work. In time, what do you think will happen with your team?
Trish:	I have to answer questions? You're not going to just *tell* me?
Coach:	I'm a coach! What do you expect?
Trish:	(Groans) Right, what was the question? In time, what do I think will happen with the team?
Coach:	That's it.
Trish:	In time, as each person is able to sort out most of their own issues, they are able to do their jobs faster because they're not waiting on me. Work is mostly being done in the right roles. If they do get stuck, they are probably better able to help each other out, so, again, not waiting on me. If they're able to do their own jobs faster, they are also able to take on additional projects and tasks, I guess.
Coach:	Absolutely, that's exactly what happens over time. What does that mean for the team and problem-solving?

Trish:	Err, well, the team is better able to sort out problems.
Coach:	What else? If they're able to sort out problems, what does that mean?
Trish:	If they are able to sort out problems, it means … that I can give them problems to sort out?
Coach:	Correct! Problems, challenging tasks or projects can be given to the team and they can collectively work through and figure it out or, at the very least, come up with some good recommendations. At that point, what type of team would you say has developed?
Trish:	I would say, at that point, they are … a high-performing team. Yes, they would be a very high-performing team at that stage.
Coach:	I think so too. And what does a high-performing team mean?
Trish:	Well, for the individual team members, it means they get exposure to additional problems, projects, and challenges that they otherwise wouldn't get experience in. Over time, that increases each of their chances of getting promoted or getting involved in opportunities that interest them. That's always a feel-good story.
Coach:	And for you?
Trish:	For me, it means I am freed up in lots of different ways. Firstly, I'm not being regularly interrupted, so I can better focus on my own tasks. Secondly, I'm not becoming a bottleneck as team members no longer need to wait for me to return from a meeting or something. Thirdly, I'm not getting overwhelmed by lots of issues to resolve or decisions to make. Fourthly, the team is able to work away, largely independent of me… Oh, the team is empowered! They know what to do and how to sort things out and have been enabled to do so. In effect, they've been empowered. I've gotten out of their way! That's it, isn't it?
Coach:	Yes, that's it. They have been empowered, both as individuals and as a team, to sort the work of the team out and deliver it, somewhat, or quite a bit, independently of you, while also keeping you informed of what is going on. If you, or the com-

pany, were focused on migrating to self-directed teams, this team could easily transition.

Trish:	That sounds like a great dynamic. I love the sound of it.
Coach:	So, if the team is empowered, and you've listed off four good things for you, what is the final positive outcome?

Trish:	Well, if I'm less busy dealing with the team's "stuff", because they're able to sort through most of it, I'm freed up to work on additional projects.
Coach:	Right, and what does that mean?

Trish:	It means that I'm also more likely to get promoted or interesting projects will come my way because I'm available and not constantly busy.
Coach:	Yep, so everyone wins. One final question—what do you think would happen to engagement within the team?

Trish:	Okay, I'm going to admit I read the *SMART Objective Setting for Managers* book so, if I remember correctly, mastery and autonomy are key elements of self-determination and motivation. In which case, everyone on the team, including me, is more likely to be motivated and engaged with their work.
Coach:	Well said. The more people have a say in how their work is organised, and solutions are implemented, the more motivated and engaged they are. Right, those are your bonus outcomes from investing your time and energy into actively developing each team member's problem-solving skills. Next stop, examining the manager's problem-solving mindset.

Trish:	I couldn't put it off forever, could I?
Coach:	Nope!

SUMMARY

There is a lot of effort required to diagnose the potential starting point, design an appropriate objective, and coach each person through the relevant problem-solving steps (or identify other, more relevant developmental objectives). However, in time, there are huge rewards, such as:

- A high-performing team that can take on additional projects and/or solve problems that might otherwise fall to the manager.
- A high-performing team tends to be a very motivated team.
- A self-directed team, able to set out and deliver their own work as assigned to the team.
- The manager is freed up to take on additional opportunities that normally neither the manager nor the team would get exposure to.
- Everyone in the team is more likely to benefit from the additional opportunities.
- The organisation, as a whole, benefits through deeper competency developed at each level within the function/organisation, reduced employee turnover and increased retention of knowledge and skills, and increased alignment between expected and actual task costs.

PROMPTS FOR YOU

Reflect on what additional benefits might accrue to you, your team and organisation.

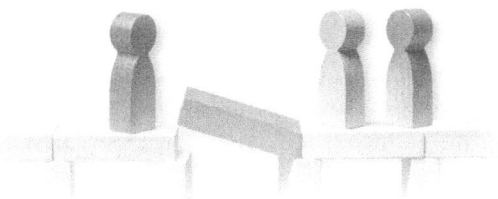

The Manager's Problem-Solving Mindset

Coach: So, Trish, now that we've had a look at the additional benefits that can accrue from empowering the team's problem-solving skills, it's finally your turn. We know you're well able to work through the various problem-solving steps.

Trish: Yes, I suppose we do.

Coach: Going back to the Attainable section of SMART, one of the things we recognised was the need for you to adjust your approach, from just jumping in and solving the issue to coaching the individual and giving them space to work through the problem-solving steps themselves.

Trish: Yes, that point has been on my mind as we've been working through each of the team members.

Coach: Great! I guess it's fair to say that your development need isn't around problem-solving but around the ability to step into a manager-as-coach style.

Trish: Okay, that makes sense. Do we just design a SMART objective for that?

Coach: We could do, but it wouldn't be my suggested starting point. The ability to step into that manager-as-coach role depends on two things. The first aspect is whether your beliefs and thoughts support the process of stepping into the role. The second aspect is whether you have the skills to step into the role.

Trish: What do you mean by the "beliefs and thoughts" to step into the role?

Coach: Well, we act off our thoughts. For example, if I have a thought that I'm hungry, I will go and get something to eat. I have a thought and then I choose whether to action it or not. If the desire to achieve the outcome is sufficiently compelling, I'm more likely to action it. If it isn't sufficiently compelling or some other thoughts creep in, I might not action it.

In our case, if I think that it's a good idea to step into the manager-as-coach role, I will take actions, such as "ask questions" rather than "give answers". As I change my action, I'm likely to get a different response from others. If I continue to give answers, I will get compliance and more escalations. If I ask questions, I am more likely to get understanding and increased likelihood that the other person knows what to do themselves next time. So, the action I take influences the outcome I get, maybe not immediately, but if I keep doing it, those around me will get used to the new approach and over time they'll respond differently. Does that make sense?

Trish: I think so.

Coach: Good. So, the next question is: where do our thoughts come from? They bubble up from our beliefs, assumptions, and values, whether we are consciously aware of them or not. As we saw with the Manager's Dilemma, if we believe our value to the organisation comes from our ability to sort out issues and problems, then when an issue is presented, the thought is likely to be something along the lines of, *I need to sort this issue out,* so our subsequent action is somewhere in the space of "giving the answer" or "taking it on, to sort out".

Trish:	Oh yes, I remember you touched on that in The Manager's Dilemma chapter. So, what *would* be your starting point?
Coach:	Great question! I would start with exploring the manager's mindset and what might be going on there. Given the complexity of the human, we can only cover so much, but we're going to explore some of the more common patterns that can arise and see if any of them resonate with you. Then we'll look at the key skills required to step into the manager-as-coach role.
Trish:	Okay. Are you going to ask the questions, to guide me?
Coach:	Yes, you did such a great job with the team that I know you'll be well able to do this. Just keep in mind it might feel a bit more uncomfortable because it's you we're talking about.
Trish:	That thought has crossed my mind! (Laughs). But I can see how my working day will improve substantially if I can make the required changes, so I'm up for the challenge.
Coach:	Brilliant, let's go! Right, so the first aspect we're going to explore is in the worldview space.
Trish:	Okay, back up, what do you mean by "worldview"?
Coach:	By "worldview", I mean the way in which we see and understand the world. For example, the Scarcity Mentality is a worldview whereby a person views the resources of the world or company as "fixed", meaning there's only so much to share out.
Trish:	Ah, I've heard of the Scarcity Mentality. That makes sense in relation to worldview.
Coach:	Good. So, for a manager with the Scarcity Mentality, what thoughts might arise from that worldview?
Trish:	Err, well, for a manager who thinks there's a fixed amount of pie, then if one person gets more, everyone else has to get less. So that worldview would naturally introduce competition within the team, function or company, depending on how senior the manager was.

Coach:	Well said. Would such a manager be *more* likely or *less* likely to help team members develop their abilities?
Trish:	Less likely, for sure. That saying "zero-sum game" springs to mind.
Coach:	Spot on! For someone with the Scarcity Mentality, if someone gets a bigger slice of a "fixed pie", it means someone else (or several other people) has to get less. It all has to tot up to the fixed amount available.
Trish:	Is it possible to change that worldview?
Coach:	I always go back to how we acquired notions such as Worldview, Personal Values, Beliefs, etc. We weren't born with them, so we had to acquire them somehow. If we acquired them, by implication, we could have acquired other versions. To me, this implies we can recognise them, change them or alter them in some way.
Trish:	How would you go about that?
Coach:	It usually starts with examining the beliefs that might underpin the worldview. It requires patience, persistence and working with someone who knows what they're doing and has the skill to tease it out.
Trish:	Is that the sound of a coaching session, I hear?
Coach:	Yes, it is! It's beyond the scope of this book. The important takeaway is that it *is* possible to shift and adjust one's worldview, to change their mindset and related behaviours, and get different outcomes. Okay, so we saw how the Scarcity Mentality worldview can negatively impact our ability to develop the team's problem-solving skills effectively. Are there any other worldviews that you can think of that might similarly undermine the manager?
Trish:	Well, a common refrain from senior managers around here is, "*I* had to figure it out myself so, *you* can figure it out yourself!" Is that a worldview?
Coach:	Excellent, we could call this the Sink-or-Swim worldview. If we throw them in the deep end and they swim, they're a good

Trish:

fit. If they sink, they're not for us! What impact does this have on the team?

Sink-or-swim…I like it! I suspect there's a lot of paddling going on around here! Well, on the face of it, I suppose the manager is less likely to take the work away from the individual. They might just give an instruction or two and leave the individual to figure out the rest of it themselves.

Coach:

Yes, that's how it could manifest itself. How is the individual likely to react to that?

Trish:

For a "swim"-type person, they'd probably go off and try to figure it out. They might eventually get there, but they might have wasted a lot of time and resources. Also, they might not follow the process or procedure, if there is one. Over time, they either absorb that way of doing things or they might get frustrated and leave, particularly if the manager starts questioning the solution.

Coach:

Well said. If we then layer on the scenario whereby this person is training a new team member, the issues start compounding! What might happen with the "sink"-type person?

Trish:

The "sink"-type person is likely to just not do the task or does it as far as they can and then leaves the rest. So, shoddy work, feeling very out of their depth, unlikely to ask for additional work and probably tries to dodge as much work as they can, to avoid feeling inadequate. Probably won't last too long!

Coach:

You're right; they probably *won't* last too long! I could imagine a couple of years into their role, if they're still there, they're likely to be quite negative, putting down new ideas, heading them off at the pass because they don't want to be exposed! Do you want to sum up the impact of a Sink-or-Swim worldview on a manager's approach to developing the team's problem-solving skills?

Trish:

I imagine that they would just expect people to figure things out themselves so wouldn't give the person much time or explain the context. They wouldn't see it as part of their responsibility to ensure their team members are trained or enabled. I also imagine that it would be very difficult for someone with this worldview to step into a manager-as-coach role as they wouldn't see the need for it. They might get rather impatient when asked for help or support.

Coach: That's really good. Let's see if we can identify one more worldview. Any thoughts?

Trish: Well, you know that saying that some people "prefer to be right than to do the right thing"? Is that a worldview?

Coach: Oh, nice one! I'd call that the "I'm Right, you're Wrong" worldview, which could be a summary of the saying. I also think it shows up often enough for us to explore it in our context. How might this impact a manager's ability to empower their team's problem-solving?

Trish: I imagine it would take quite a while for a manager with this worldview to trust that someone else could do it as well as them or that their solution would be as good as the manager's own solution.

I could also imagine that they would question someone else's solution as an automatic reaction. There would be constant signalling that it would be a good idea to take the manager's solution as the way to proceed. Even for a very capable and competent person, this would wear thin after a while. Their confidence would be knocked and they would just end up acquiescing because it would be easier.

Coach: To summarise, the actions arising from this worldview are likely to disempower a team, even one that has been empowered!

Trish: That's it, in a nutshell!

Coach: As I mentioned earlier, there are many worldviews and they inform our beliefs which, in turn, inform our thoughts. Bringing this back to yourself, Trish, do you have any sense of what your worldview is?

Trish: Oh … eh … I'm not sure if I do have a sense of what my worldview is. From discussing the ones we touched on, I don't think any of those resonated with me. Maybe I'm more in the space of "wanting to be liked". Is that a worldview?

Coach: Ooh, there's a good one—wanting to be liked! I don't know if, strictly speaking, it would be considered a worldview, but it's a good point to explore. What worldview do you think might inform this thought?

Trish: Well, I feel rather uncomfortable handing work back to someone or giving them work to do. So when I say, "I want to be liked", it's in that context of not feeling comfortable in giving other people work. Is my worldview about seeing myself as equal to others?

Coach: That could well be your worldview. Let's explore the "wanting to be liked" bit. How does that show up for you?

Trish: Within me, it shows up as a knotty feeling in my stomach. I think I shouldn't give the team work that I wouldn't do myself. When they come to me with a question, I think that by answering it I'm being nice and that they'll like me if I'm helpful. Now, though, from all the work we've done, I can see that my role isn't the same as the roles within the team. I'm not being paid to do the same work as the team.

Coach: Well done! It's brilliant that you can see the beliefs that have been driving your actions. It's also great that you can now see that the worldview and/or assumptions you had made are not necessarily appropriate for your new role.

Trish: Yes, the biggest realisation is that I thought I was being helpful, but actually I was holding back each person's development in their role. Ultimately, I was holding back their careers. How long would you continue to like a person if they were actually holding you back, no matter how nice or helpful they seemed to be?

Coach: Ironic, isn't it?

Trish:	Very!
Coach:	So, it's fair to say you've had some level of a realisation about your beliefs, worldviews, assumptions, and actions.
Trish:	Definitely!
Coach:	Here's my curiosity coming out here, but can I ask you another question?
Trish:	Go on...
Coach:	In terms of the way you have been acting with the team, what was your intention?
Trish:	My intention?
Coach:	Yes, your beliefs and actions are one thing. But what was your intention? What did you intend to happen?
Trish:	My intention was to be a good manager, helping the team get their work done.
Coach:	Right. If you had to classify your intentions, would you say they were good, bad, or indifferent?
Trish:	They were good ... my intention was to do right by the team.
Coach:	I thought you'd say that. Why do you think I'm asking about your intentions?
Trish:	Err ... well ... I suppose you're asking because we might behave in ways that... No, I don't really know. Why are you asking about them?
Coach:	Now there's an honest answer! I'm asking because, from your perspective, your intentions are to do the right thing by the team members. However, due to beliefs, assumptions and thoughts, your actions were resulting in a different outcome for the team! While you intended to help them, they were actually being disempowered. You know the old saying "people leave managers, not jobs"?
Trish:	Yes! Doesn't everybody?

Coach:	Well, if you ask people who are managers, the vast majority of them will say that their intentions, as a manager, towards their team are good. Most managers don't go out of their way to irritate, annoy or demotivate people. Would that be fair to say?
Trish:	This is starting to feel like that philosophy class I took in college—nobody would say they're boring, would they?
Coach:	Quite! Well, nobody *would* say they're boring! And you're on the right track with that comparison! Most people don't intentionally go out of their way to upset or hurt people and most managers don't go into work every day with the intention to demotivate and hold back their people.
Trish:	No, you're right. Logically, the vast majority of managers wouldn't intentionally do that.
Coach:	Yet, we have the old saying "people leave managers, not jobs". My point here is that, while we might have good intentions, how we actually outwardly behave, i.e. our actions, is often informed by our beliefs, thoughts, assumptions and worldviews and they might result in outcomes that are different to our intentions.
Trish:	How are we supposed to figure all *this* out?
Coach:	Good question! That, in a nutshell, is why self-awareness is such a cornerstone of effective management and leadership! So guess what *that* means?
Trish:	I'm thinking it means it's beyond the scope of this book and the need for a few one-to-one coaching sessions?
Coach:	That topic is definitely beyond the scope of this book! Coaching is optional, but if you want to speed up the learning, then yes, coaching would be the fastest way. Reading or listening to self-help books in this space and actively and honestly doing the exercises and some good old self-reflection is an alternative way to go.
Trish:	Hmm, that's some food for thought! Right, if I summarise what we've covered so far, our worldviews impact our beliefs and thoughts and that shows up in our actions and behaviours.

Other people respond to our actions and behaviours, presumably through the lenses of their own worldviews and beliefs, and we get outcomes. There can be initial outcomes and then there can be outcomes that build up over a period of time. Our actions and behaviours might not appear to match our intentions. To be better able to align our intentions with our actions, we need a pretty decent level of self-awareness, which takes a bit of work and a lot of commitment. Does that cover it?

Coach: That's a pretty good round-up.

Trish: Do we need to set an objective for me, around changing my belief?

Coach: Here's the funny thing. Every time I've done the beliefs thing with someone and they've uncovered the belief that's been driving them, there's this huge "ah-ha" moment. When we catch up at the start of our next coaching session, the belief seems to have mysteriously vanished. It's like exposing the belief causes it to evaporate into a plume of smoke, never to be seen again. When I probe, the individual's behaviour has changed because their thoughts have changed and they're getting different, more helpful outcomes.

Trish: Really?

Coach: Yes, really! After the first few times, I actually started asking people what happened to their old belief. Eaten bread is soon forgotten and so, it would seem, is an exposed belief because they kinda look at me with a "what are you talking about?" look! From what I can conclude, they didn't actively or consciously do anything about the belief. It was just gone, like a puff of smoke.

Why am I telling you all that? It's so that you'll understand that I'm going to suggest that we don't need to set an objective in this space. If we have uncovered the belief that's been undermining your ability to actively develop and empower the team, your thoughts and actions should naturally change and we don't

Trish: really need to do anything else about it. However, I would recommend you monitor it yourself. If you feel there's something else there, then we will need to uncover and deal with that issue.

Trish: Okay, given what you've experienced, that makes sense. Are we done with the manager's mindset or is there more?

Coach: There's a bit more. I'm going to save the best for last so I think we'll take a quick look at our personal values and how they might undermine a manager's mindset in relation to developing other people's problem-solving.

Trish: Values? I thought they were supposed to be inherently "good"!

Coach: A good observation. Values do tend to be held up as the Nirvana of goodness, but in reality, values are actually fairly neutral. They are beliefs that certain concepts are very important to us and that we expect ourselves, and others, to uphold them. The lofty ones of Trust and Integrity often get trotted out, but oftentimes people actually hold personal values such as Efficiency or even Conflict-Avoidance.

Trish: Really?

Coach: Yes, when you actually get up and personal to understanding a person's values, what is actually important to them can be quite niche!

Trish: I had no idea!

Coach: Of course, they might be encased in assumptions and expectations within the general societal values they grew up in, but their specific personal values can be pretty niche.

Trish: Okay, so what do we need to explore in relation to my values, my mindset and developing others' problem-solving skills?

Coach: There's one value in particular that can hugely impact a manager's ability to empower their team and that is the value of Perfection. From working with several managers with this value, it often shows up as the need for "control". If we think about it, a person with a value of Perfection has an expectation that tasks are completed "perfectly"—well, their definition of "perfectly", at any rate.

This tends to show up in two different ways. Either they just pretty much do everything themselves, in which case they don't take the time to develop and empower their team members, or they give the work to someone to do and then focus in on the last 2% that wasn't done *exactly* right and nit-pick. Over time, this erodes the other person's confidence and they often stop trying because, after all, what's the point? It's going to be wrong anyway!

Trish: Ooh, that doesn't sound like much fun *at all!*

Coach: You're right, it's not much fun, neither for the team member nor for the manager themselves.

Trish: Well, on the bright side, I don't think Perfection is something I need to worry about!

Coach: Well, that answers that question then!

Trish: No, but if this *was* something relevant to me, *would* it be possible to change my value of Perfection?

Coach: Great question and the answer is that it's a bit of a mix. I've worked with some managers who have been able to train themselves to approach situations in a different way. For example, for a manager who always focused on the 2% wrong, they were able to reframe things so that they could acknowledge the 98% that was correct and frame the impact of the 2% in a more positive way.

With another person, we explored and categorised tasks into which ones absolutely had to be done right 100% of the time and which ones were acceptable at 90% done.

Trish: Is there a difference?

Coach: Well, yes. For example, a pilot needs to land a plane successfully 100% of the time, but writing up a report 90% correctly might

	well be sufficient. In that case, literally nobody is going to die from a report that is completed to a 90% standard.
Trish:	Okay, I can see how different tasks might need a different level of finish.
Coach:	Just to finish off the answer to your question, coaching will work as a means for many people to reframe their expectations arising from a value of Perfection, but it won't work with everyone. Some people have underlying challenges that contribute to the Perfection.
Trish:	I'll take your word on that! Are there any other values that might hijack a manager's mindset?
Coach:	Well, I mentioned that some people have a value of Efficiency. Depending on how they defined their value, they could see that just sorting out the issue themselves is more efficient that coaching someone else. In that case, it's not so much the "having a value of Efficiency" that is causing the issue; it's how they are defining the meaning of that value.
	Since I mentioned Trust as a value, Trust also has the potential to cause mischief! Although not necessarily Trust as a value!
Trish:	I'm a little confused here? Trust, as a value but not really?
Coach:	Yeah, this is a little confusing. Not everyone elevates Trust to a value, but we all have views on "Trust" and how it emerges. Leaving aside the idea of Trust as a value and focusing on the general concept of trust, I have found that people typically fall into one of two categories; either they extend trust to others, until proven otherwise, or they require other people to earn their trust. For a person who believes that trust must be earned, they are less likely to make the leap into developing other people's problem-solving skills until they trust the person.
Trish:	Oh my, there's a lot to this! In short, what do I need to know?
Coach:	Good idea, let's just get to the bottom line! The question you need to answer is: do you naturally trust that if you give a per-

son a task with some direction, if they need it, they will be able to reasonably complete the task? Or do you expect that they won't be able to do it?

Trish: I think I expect that they'll be able to do it... Yes, when I gave Lisa a piece of work the other day, I thought she would be able to do it.

Coach: That would be my sense too. If people needed to earn your trust, I think that would have come out more prominently in how you answered some of the questions posed as we were working through the different team members.

Trish: So, if it turned out that people had to earn my trust, what would that mean?

Coach: Well, depending on how you wanted to approach it, it would mean exploring the cost of people having to earn your trust and if the cost was worth paying. That could result in designing a process to increase the chances of people earning your trust and/or reframing the belief. If you had a worldview of "I'm right", chances are you'd just stick with the belief and pay the costs. In summary, it would mean that there would be a body of work to do to explore the issue and how best to proceed.

Trish: Yes, that makes sense.

Coach: Okay, that's enough about values and trust. Let's move on to the really fun stuff, or what I like to call the Emotional Kick.

Trish: The Emotional Kick?

Coach: Yes, the Emotional Kick! This is the emotional feel-good factor some people get from "sorting things out". Some people's identities are wrapped up in their "thing". It translates to "I'm good at...", "my superpower is...", "I add value by..."

For a manager who sees their superpower as getting into the middle of issues and sorting them out, they get an immediate "feel good" kick every time they sort an issue out. In fact, the more they seem to be needed to sort things out the better they feel. From their emotional and self-value perspectives, they have absolutely zero interest in empowering their team because empowering their team would take away opportunities to use their superpower and feel good about themselves. How easy do you think it would be to give *that* up?

Trish: Very difficult.

Coach: Or how about revelling in the hustle and bustle of fire-fighting? For a manager who gets a kick out of the excitement of swooping in and sorting out a fire, they might quite like not having the team fully trained or empowered. That's not to say they won't moan and groan about the inconvenience of it all! Ah, the contradictions of the human! Love a good ol' moan but no interest in trying to change it!

Trish: Yes, I've come across a few of those people in my career!

Coach: Does the "Emotional Kick" descriptor make sense now?

Trish: Absolutely! I have definitely seen both those patterns of behaviour show up in different teams.

Coach: I'd say most people have experienced them at some point! While there are other examples of the Emotional Kick, I'd say the "centre of action" and "fire fighter" emotional kicks are probably amongst the most common examples. Either of those resonate with you?

Trish: Well, there's a chance I enjoy a bit of the "centre of action" one. I don't think I'm totally addicted, *yet*, so maybe there's hope for me?

Coach: (Laughs) Fair play that you're acknowledging the possibility. It's not an easy thing to admit.

Trish: What should I do about it? Is this my own developmental objective?

Coach: It could be. What would you need to do to break this habit or to stop it getting more embedded?

Trish:	Err, well, I guess I would need to observe whether there is truth to my suspicion.
Coach:	Okay, so what would that look like?
Trish:	Well, I could examine my emotional response to issues being brought to me.
Coach:	Good idea. How would you do that?
Trish:	I could take time to reflect on what emotions are showing up for me and where they're showing up. Like, if my suspicion is correct, I should feel excitement, which usually shows up as a burst of energy for me. I also get butterflies in my stomach when I'm excited.
Coach:	That sounds good. In the event that you're correct, what would you need to do to break the habit?
Trish:	I think I would need to reframe my thoughts towards getting excited at the opportunity to develop the team member rather than my sorting out of the issue. So, I need to get an emotional kick out of my superpower being "seeing the team grow" or "empowering my team", or something like that!
Coach:	That's a great way of reframing it, redefining the source of your emotional kick. To help you along the way, what would the benefit of that be?
Trish:	How do you mean?
Coach:	Let's go back to the fire-fighting manager. Long-term, what do you think happens to that manager?
Trish:	Long-term? Well, if you're constantly fire-fighting, you're very busy. So, people are less likely to ask you to get involved in other projects and you miss out on opportunities. Over time, opportunities and promotions are more likely to go to others as they were involved in and got experience in other areas. So, long-term, such a manager is likely to get stuck there!

Coach:	That's a good depiction of how it often works out. The other, even more damaging route is they get promoted and cause even more fire-fighting, but let's not go there today! So, going back to the question of the benefit of getting an emotional kick from developing and empowering the team, what might that look like over time?
Trish:	Okay, I get this question now! If the team is empowered, we get the high-performing team, the increased spare capacity, so the increased likelihood of getting exposure to additional or strategic projects, which then increases the likelihood of additional opportunities arising. So valuing this emotional kick benefits everyone, not just the manager. Got it!
Coach:	Have you really gotten it? I ask because there's the cognitive "yes, my brain gets this" and there's the emotional "aha" moment, which is where the real long-term shift happens.
Trish:	I think no, better yet I *feel* that I've had that "aha" moment. I truly am committed to working with the team, to support them in their own development and coach them through the different steps. I can actually feel the excitement growing!
Coach:	Oh, and where is it showing up?
Trish:	Like I said, I'm feeling a burst of energy and I'm all revved up to get going!
Coach:	Well done, that's brilliant to hear. Do we need an actual objective for you?
Trish:	No, I think I'm good. After all, I've acknowledged my objective in every one of my team members' objectives, under Attainable. That's my commitment to their success.

SUMMARY

The manager's mindset has a huge impact on how they view themselves and their team and how they approach delivering their role, as manager. Having a clear awareness of what shapes our mindset and how that drives our thoughts, actions, behaviours and outcomes is very important to being a manager that can empower their team.

There are many different inputs to our mindset, including:

- Worldview & related beliefs
- Personal Values
- Emotional Kicks

Mindset is not static. If we understand the drivers of it and adjust, change or reframe unhelpful drivers, our mindset changes. As a result, our thoughts change, so our actions change and we get different outcomes. We have a choice to make. Stay as we are and continue to get the results we have always gotten or commit to putting in the work needed to change and access the benefits available?

PROMPTS FOR YOU

Return to the completed Manager's Problem-Solving Mindset worksheet, or wherever you jotted down your answers to the questions posed in the Introduction. Re-read your answers, consider them in light of reading this chapter and identify if they align with any of the worldviews, emotional kicks, values and/or approaches to trust explored.

Review each of the mindset drivers, reflect on them and for each one articulate what your specific story is. For example, articulate your worldview or your beliefs. If none of the worldviews touched on resonated with you, you may need to do some research on examples of other possible worldviews.

Regardless of what level of management you are at, once completed, reflect on whether each driver is of use to you or if it is undermining you in the following:

- your role as manager
- your ability to empower your team's problem-solving

If you suspect a driver is undermining you, reflect on what you are committed to doing to adjust, change or reframe that mindset driver. What support would you need to make those changes? Where and how would you get that support?

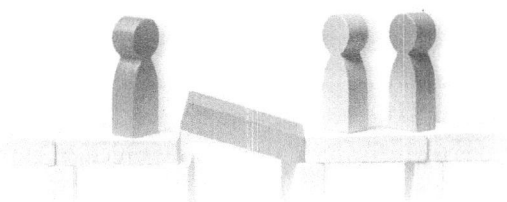

Introducing the New Escalation Approach

How are you going to go about introducing this new approach to your team?

Coach: Trish, can you believe it, we're on the homeward stretch! All we need to do now is decide on the best way to introduce this new approach, to escalation, to the team.

Trish: Ooh, it's getting very real now!

Coach: It sure is! Before we go into planning how you're going to introduce it, let's first recap on what we're talking about when we say "new approach". If you recall from Chapter Six: Designing a Generic Problem-Solving Objective, we're talking about two specific aspects. Firstly, when they bring an issue to you, what's their ask? Can you remember what the three options were?

Trish: Oh right, it's been a while! The three valid reasons for escalation are:
    a. They need help and/or a sounding board
    b. It's a true escalation, i.e. they have done everything they could to resolve it and now it needs to be escalated to the next level up
    c. They are keeping me in the loop

Coach: That's it. The second aspect we're talking about is what we expect them to have done in advance of coming to you with an escalation that falls into category a: needing help and/or a sounding board.

What we're seeking to do here is signpost to the team that your expectations have changed; that they are still welcome to bring issues to you but, when they do, they need to tell you:
  i. For which of the three valid escalation reasons they are bringing the issue to you
  ii. If they are looking for help, they need to have sized the impact of the issue, researched it, identified and explored possible solution, at a minimum.

Trish: But what if they're starting from an earlier step? What if they don't know how to identify possible solutions?

Coach: Good question. What we're looking at doing with this initial signposting is laying out your stall as to what the end goal will look like, i.e. they are more than welcome to bring issues and problems to you but you do expect a certain amount of the ground work to be done and this is the expectation of everyone on the team. You will need to acknowledge that this is the desired end point but that some people will need to build up to being able to meet that expectation.

Trish: Ah, that makes more sense. So, there's the initial setting out what the end expectation is and then there's acknowledging people's individual starting points. Is that it?

Coach: Yes, that's it.

Trish: And do I acknowledge people's starting points when I'm setting out my stall?

Coach: Well Trish, that would depend on several factors such as: are you introducing and setting out your stall with the team in a team meeting or on an individual basis? Is everyone starting from a similar starting point or are some people able to meet the expectation right away while others aren't?

Trish: Yes, I can see why taking those points into consideration might be necessary or I could seriously put my foot in it. I can't imagine Merv or Damon would appreciate me highlighting their starting points to the rest of the team!

Coach: No, I can't imagine they'd thank you for that. The other thing to consider is whether you introduce the new approach formally, through the Objective-Setting process, or informally, at some point during the year. What might you want to consider here?

Trish: Err, I suppose I would consider how near we are to the objective-setting season and how long I can wait.

Coach: That is a pretty succinct summary of the key points to consider. If you're near enough to the objective-setting period and you're not in desperate straits, you could hold off and introduce it as a new way of working, as part of performance development. On the other hand, if it's too long to wait and you need to introduce it sooner, a more informal introduction might be appropriate. What would you imagine the difference between the formal and informal approaches might be?

Trish: Well, with both approaches I think there would likely need to be a signposting meeting, where I set out my stall and they're all hearing the same message and they know that it's for all of us, rather than some people thinking it's just them.

Coach: I'd agree with you there.

Trish: Then I think with the formal approach, as part of the objective-setting process, I'd be exploring their starting point and we would formally agree a developmental objective, along the lines we covered out in Chapters Seven to Ten.

Coach: Yep.

Trish: With the informal approach, I guess I wouldn't be formally setting out an objective with them, but, using the diagnostic work I've already done, I'd probably start coaching them from where I suspect their starting point is. Maybe as part of the team meeting, introducing the concept, I'd go through the eight steps of problem-solving, so we both have that agreed framework to work from.

Coach: That's an excellent idea. To recap, as part of the general team meeting, you'd introduce the three valid reasons for escalation and the eight steps of problem-solving and then set out which steps you would expect to have been completed prior to escalating an issue for the reason of needing help/sounding board. Is that it?

Trish: Yes, that's it. Actually, I could use the definitions outlined in Chapter Three: The Steps of Problem-Solving to discuss and explore what we, as a team, mean by each step, so that we're all on the same page as to what each of the steps do and don't mean for our team and our work.

Coach: Sounds like a short workshop has just been planned out.

Trish: Great. Is there anything else I would need to be aware of or think about?

Coach: If you're going the formal route, you would naturally discuss their starting point with them as part of agreeing their developmental objective. If you go the informal route, your preparation work will give you a sense of where you think each person's starting point is, but will that necessarily be correct?

Trish: Err, I suppose it wouldn't necessarily be correct. I could have misinterpreted the observable behaviours.

Coach: Right, and of course they'll have their own perspective as to what is causing their pattern of behaviour. It could be that the way they are behaving is a response to your behaviour.

Trish: Oh, yeah, I hadn't thought of that. That could be tricky! I could get all sorts of kick-back.

Coach: You sure could! So if you choose the informal route, what could you do to ensure this scenario doesn't turn into reality?

Trish: I suppose I could arrange a one-to-one meeting with each of them and ask some reflective and probing questions to establish where they're really starting from. At least if we can agree which step they find themselves starting to struggle with, we can discuss how I can support and coach them.

Coach: That sounds like a good idea. And of course, if they think they're very good at a step while your analysis has indicated that you suspect they struggle with it, you can ask probing questions to get them to reflect a bit deeper. Just have some examples ready in your back pocket!

Trish: How do you mean?

Coach: Well, if Merv thinks he's great at evaluating the size of a problem, which is step two, and instead he thinks it's identifying options (step four), you would need to ask some questions that prompt him to reflect on if and how he determines the size of an issue. To do that effectively, it's good to have a few recent examples that you can pull out and examine, through the lens of curiosity of course.

Trish: Of course! Am I correct in saying that while I can introduce the new approach at any time of the year, the real difference between a "formal" introduction as part of objective setting and an "informal" introduction at some point during the year is that I would actually share the SMART objective with them and formally capture it if I'm introducing it as part of objective setting?

Coach: That's it. Ideally, everything else would still be done. So, the analysis and preparation you did in Chapter Five: Diagnosing the Starting Point, mapping out relevant developmental plans you covered out during Chapters Seven to Ten, the team meeting to introduce the new expectations and approach that we've covered out in this chapter and the one-to-one meetings to help both of you understand each individual's starting point would all still need to happen. If you go the informal route, you would probably then just start coaching them from their starting point.

Trish: Would I need to readjust my starting point?

| Coach: | Do you mean in the event that where you *thought* their starting point was turned out to be different to where it *actually* was? |
| Trish: | Yes. |

| Coach: | In that situation, yes, you would need to adjust your starting point. |
| Trish: | That's what I thought. |

| Coach: | One final point. They need to change as do you. By this I mean that if they come up to you with an issue, you need to hold the line in relation to them categorising the purpose for the escalation and you also need to avoid reverting to type and just giving them the answer or taking the issue from them. Right? |
| Trish: | Eh, yes, right! |

| Coach: | When you're introducing the new approach in the team meeting, you will need to acknowledge that everyone, including you, will have to adjust, which will take a bit of time to get used to. I'd recommend you agree a safe word or phrase that everyone within the team can use to highlight that the new approach has been breached. So, if Carla comes to you and launches straight in, you can use the word or phrase to remind her to start with the escalation category. Much more importantly, if you jump straight in, trying to solve the issue, they have a safe way of reminding you and bringing it to your attention. |
| Trish: | Oh, yeah, that makes a lot of sense. How do I pick a safe word? |

| Coach: | I'd suggest you introduce the idea and let the team decide on the word or phrase. |
| Trish: | Okay. |

| Coach: | So? |
| Trish: | So? |

| Coach: | So, what have you decided? Are you going to wait until the objective setting or start straightaway? |

Trish: What do you think? Start straightaway, of course! I'm not wait-
           ing for another three months. We'll practically be a high-per-
           forming team by then!
Coach: That's what I like to hear!

SUMMARY

This new approach to escalation and developing the team's problem-solving skills can be introduced either formally, as part of the objective-setting process, or informally during the year. Either way, a team meeting to introduce the three valid reasons to escalate, the eight steps to problem-solving and the shift in expectations should happen. In addition, acknowledging that the change will take a while to bed in and that everyone, including the manager, will need to shift their approach is important.

Finally, agreeing a mechanism to call out breaches in adherence, whether by an individual team member or the manager, is important. This ensures that everyone in the team feels that it's not just them, that the *whole* team is in it together and that the team can hold the manager to account as much as the manager can hold the team members to account.

PROMPTS FOR YOU

Think about when and how you're going to introduce the new approach to your team. Does the formal or informal approach work better? Examine your mindset and see if you are comfortable in being held accountable by the team for the changes you need to make. If that idea makes you feel uncomfortable, revisit Chapter Twelve: The Manager's Problem-Solving Mindset and try to examine what might be prompting your source of discomfort.

CONCLUSION

Most managers, when asked, would say that they would love to have an empowered team. A team confident in sorting out many of the routine issues that arise within teams. A team that regularly demonstrates good judgement on what to resolve themselves and what to escalate and always keeps their manager in the loop. What's not to like?

As we have seen throughout this book, there is a complexity to achieving such an empowered team. As a manager, there's the need to recognise that it's no longer about you, it's all about the team. As we saw with Jaime, do they have the knowledge and skills to do their job in the first place? Do they know it well enough to know what's important and what's not so important, like we saw with Merv? Has their knowledge deepened sufficiently for them to be able to research the issues and identify potential solutions? This is where we saw Damon struggle.

As complex as the issues were with Merv, Jaime and Damon, they were the easy ones because their issues dealt with knowledge and skills. Knowledge and skills are relatively easy to sort out. As we move towards Lisa's, Ericka's and Carla's developmental needs, we see a rapid increase in complexity. Here, we're dealing with issues of confidence and trust. With Carla, we're getting into the need to understand the various aspects of emotional intelligence and how they manifest themselves in people's behaviour. This is a level of complexity that many, if not most, managers don't have the knowledge or experience to recognise.

Finally, as if the last two paragraphs didn't depict enough complexity, there's the question of how the manager shows up in the team. The manager has put in the hard work and been rewarded with a promotion, often on the basis of being good at "sorting things out", aka problem-solving. Can they recognise that their role has changed? That they are there to enable the team to do much of the work of the team and that, as manager, they will still be rewarded? Not as an individual contributor who is good at problem-solving, but as a manager who has invested the time and effort to build up a pretty amazing team that can sort out *lots* of issues!

That's just the start of it, though, for the manager. Even if their brain is shouting out, I'*m ready for this! I'm ready for this NOW!*, as we have seen, emotionally they may not be ready. There may be all sorts of intangibles that are holding them back—a personal value, a worldview, an emotional kick.

Ironically enough, the easiest part of all this may actually be recognising and introducing the three valid reasons to escalate, namely: a true escalation, needing help/sounding board or keeping the manager in the loop. Introducing the reasons, setting out the expectations and then making a concerted effort to ensure that you pause long enough to build out the habit within the team may actually be, relatively speaking, more straightforward.

If you grapple with knowing how to empower your team, freeing up your own time and being able to take advantage of opportunities, you are not alone. This book was written to help you understand the complexity of the potential dynamics that might be showing up within both you and your team. Of course, understanding the complexity isn't enough. I also wanted to provide you with a practical way to diagnose where an individual's starting point in problem-solving may be and how you can devise a developmental plan to coach them through the remaining steps.

Since complexity of the human is involved, this will take an investment of time, personal learning and effort. You may recognise that you need your own coaching support. You will definitely need to put time and effort into reflecting on where each of your team members is in relation to their ability to sort out issues and creating an individual development plan. However, the potential rewards are huge. Your team members can become super competent and confident problem-solvers, increasing their individual and collective performance. You get more time to focus on the added-value aspects of your role. All of you increase your career opportunities. There's a lot of upside to this investment. Are you ready?

WHAT ARE MY NEXT STEPS?

Congratulations on finishing this book. I hope you enjoyed it and gained some useful insights into problem-solving and the dynamics within your own team. I am always fascinated by the impact of our thoughts and actions on the dynamics that result in outcomes. Without realising it, we can contribute to the very situations we don't like; and I speak from personal experience! By writing this book, I hope I can help thousands more managers understand these subtleties, break the dynamics and empower their teams to higher levels of performance, job satisfaction and career opportunities.

As you have likely concluded yourself, the whole area of problem-solving, coaching others to be able to resolve their own issues and how we approach escalation combine into a very subtle subject. I hope I have done justice to deconstructing the strands and providing you with a practical framework to use with your team. I'd love to hear your own stories of how you approach changing your team's dynamics and the outcomes that arise. Please feel free to reach out to me on LinkedIn or email me at irial.ofarrell@evolutioncon-sulting.ie.

So now it's up to you to decide what you're going to do next. How are you going to introduce this new approach? What changes will *you* need to make, to ensure this new approach works? What changes are your team going to have to make? What supports will be required?

I strongly suggest you map out a plan and start working through it. The plan will likely include:

- Analysis of team
- Analysis of your own problem-solving mindset
- Identifying development coaching plan for each team member
- Determining best time and manner of introducing the new approach

- Identifying any additional supports required
- Getting approval for additional supports identified.

If you feel you could do with some additional guidance, I'd be delighted to support you in any of the following ways:

- Working directly with you, as the manager, to tease out exactly what is happening within the team and design potential coaching plans for each team member.
- Working with the team, to facilitate a team workshop, to introduce and explore the concepts of problem-solving, escalation, etc.
- Providing one-to-one coaching to a team member, to work through a specific issue that has been identified as part of this process.

Please feel free to drop me an email, irial.ofarrell@evolutionconsulting.ie, to discussion how I can help you with empowering your team's problem-solving. Alternatively, book an Executive Coaching session or an Executive Reflection program at www.evolutionconsutling.ie.

"What is an Executive Reflection program?", I hear you ask. An excellent question! Through delivering both executive leadership development programs and executive coaching, I regularly find myself discussing the need to "take time out and reflect" with leaders and managers alike. Their response is usually something along the lines of "I know I should but…I don't have time". The Executive Reflection program is designed to ensure that reflection time is inserted into your week. The program consists of 12 x 45-minute meetings, scheduled weekly or bi-weekly. Each week, you bring the situation you want to reflect on and I bring the questions and the curiosity. Together, we unpick what *exactly* is going on, what your options are and your next steps. Before you ask, it differs from Executive Coaching, as the focus is on the situation, rather than your own personal development. Although, that *may* come up, from time to time!

If you want to keep up to date on my next book, blogs, and podcasts, I'd be delighted if you signed up to my email list at www.evolutionconsulting.ie/sign-up.

It takes a bit of effort to change established team dynamics but we know it is possible. Through this book, you know exactly how to identify where you need to put your effort and what specific effort you need to apply, to empower your team's problem-solving and realise everyone's potential.

I wish you every bit of luck in doing so.

All my best,
Irial

REFERENCES

Chapter 12:
Definition of world views:
https://www.collinsdictionary.com/dictionary/english/world-view

OTHER BOOKS BY THE AUTHOR

Values—Not Just for the Office Wall Plaque:
How Personal and Company Values Intersect

Published in 2012, Irial's first book arose from her fascination with personal values and how the understanding of the concept of values profoundly changed her life. The book explains what personal values are, why they matter and the different types of low-level conflict and tension that arise within the workplace. The second part of the book explains how to articulate company values and incorporate them into company culture, to really bring them to life, rather than just pretty words on a wall plaque.

Available now on Amazon:
mybook.to/Values

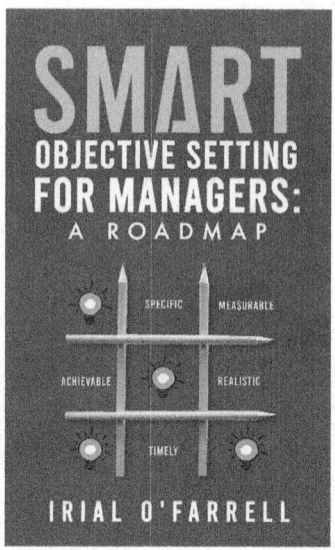

SMART Objective Setting for Managers: A Roadmap

Many managers, and their organisations, are familiar with the SMART framework for designing objectives. What is less well-known is that, when setting an objective with another person, two processes are being used: SMART and Communication. This book deconstructs the SMART framework while incorporating a deep understanding of the human, to provide a unique take on using SMART as part of the objective setting process. The book also examines how to design tangible behavioural SMART objectives such as improving communication and increasing stakeholder management.

Available now on Amazon:
Mybook.to/SMARTManagers

ACKNOWLEDGEMENTS

I'd like to thank everyone who helped me with creating this book. To my reading crew—Fergal O'Farrell, Dilis Clare and Philip Gammell—your feedback and ideas were invaluable and helped polish it. To my launch team, thanks for all your support and help, getting the word out. To Ken, my editor, thanks for all the positive words and the corrections! To everyone who gave feedback on my book cover and title, it was an iterative process, so thanks for all the ideas, particularly Mona Shah. To 100Covers, who designed the various cover options and the final version. To Keith, who is always there for me.

ABOUT THE AUTHOR

Irial lives in Dublin, Ireland, with her husband, three kids and two cats. She is fascinated with what makes people tick and she applies this through her work, working with companies and individuals to realise their potential. She loves reading (of course), learning new ideas and trying them out, travelling and quizzes. She's waiting for Covid to abate, so that she can join a quiz team someday soon.

Irial is a qualified leadership development trainer and executive coach, accredited in Insights Discovery and MHS Emotional Intelligence. She is the first, and currently only, Change Management Institute (CMI) accredited Master in Change Management in Ireland.

For more details on the full suite of services and online courses she offers, please go to www.evolutionconsulting.ie

Connect with her on: linkedin.com/in/irialofarrell
Follow her on: https://www.amazon.com/Irial-OFarrell/e/B007G
                     X1QIO
                     www.twitter.com/evolution_ary
                     https://www.facebook.com/Evolution-Consulting-
                     91352921868/
Like her books on: https://www.facebook.com/Irial-OFarrell-Books

She is currently starting to plot her next book in the Performance Development series, focused on giving effective feedback, which she is aiming to publish in 2022.

FINAL WORD

Want to help ?

FOUND THIS BOOK HELPFUL?

Did you know that reviews help other people to decide which books to buy but only 1 in 100 readers leave a review?

I wrote this book to help managers just like you to make sense of problem solving and escalation. If you found this book beneficial, it would be brilliant if you could take 2 minutes to pay it forward. How? By rating it and sharing your thoughts on your eReader, Amazon, or other chosen platform. The more reviews this book gets, the more they will help other managers to find, and benefit from, these ideas.

Thank you for taking the time.

Made in United States
North Haven, CT
11 March 2022